THE ILLUSTRATED
COURTROOM

"The best courtroom illustrations are simply those that convey most directly and honestly exactly what the artist sees." —Howard Brodie

In February 1964, Howard Brodie illustrated the courtroom where Jack Ruby, assassin of Lee Harvey Oswald, stood trial. Brodie marked this drawing to show where participants would sit, along with unusual elements of the day, like the spittoon on the right. Judge Joe G. Brown barred chewing of tobacco and cigar smoking in court during the trial.

ILLUSTRATION BY HOWARD BRODIE © ESTATE OF HOWARD BRODIE. IMAGE COURTESY OF THE LIBRARY OF CONGRESS

THE ILLUSTRATED COURTROOM

50+ YEARS OF COURT ART

2ND EDITION

ELIZABETH WILLIAMS
AND SUE RUSSELL

Redwood Publishing

First edition published by CUNY Journalism Press and printed in Canada, 2014
CUNY Journalism Press is the academic imprint of the CUNY Graduate
School of Journalism, part of the City University of New York
219 West 40th Street, New York, NY 10018
www.press.journalism.cuny.edu

Second edition published by Redwood Publishing, LLC, 2022 and printed in the United States, 2022
www.redwooddigitalpublishing.com
Orange County, California

Cataloging-in-Publication data is available from the Library of Congress.
A catalog record for this book is available from the British Library.

First Edition ISBN Information:
ISBN 978-1-939293-52-7 paperback
ISBN 978-1-939293-53-4 e-book

Second Edition ISBN Information:
ISBN 978-1-956470-42-0 hardcover
ISBN 978-1-956470-15-4 paperback
ISBN 978-1-956470-16-1 e-book

CONTENTS

This book is dedicated to the memory of Howard Brodie and Richard Tomlinson and to my parents, especially my mother, who always loved a good book.

ELIZABETH WILLIAMS

FOREWORD

By Irina Tarsis, Esq., Founder of the Center for Art Law (NYC)

Toga, sword, scales, and a blindfold. The attributes of Lady Justice impress upon courthouse visitors how the legal system is expected to function, from the ancient times: without mercy, indiscriminately, fairly. While she might be blind she is not oblivious to the spectacle that takes place in her presence. Every day when the court is in session, she witnesses a procession of characters, taking in a myriad of textures and all types and fibers of society: the cut of their suits, their haircuts, their accessories, and their facial expressions: smiles of relief, tears of regret, pallor of fear, or red-faced indignation. Public norms and personal fashion choices of named parties and anonymous actors assemble in hushed and imposing courtrooms for hearings, judgments, resolutions. Words alone cannot describe these moments or the look on one's face when they learn their verdict. Who else is there to see and depict justice in the making? Courtroom artists. Courtroom artists lend their eyes, skills, and individual aesthetics to allow the rest of us a front row view of what transpires in the courtroom. Drawings created contemporaneously with a trial complement the court record, supplant thousands of words, and distill hours of waiting, to make legal proceedings more accessible.

Courtroom illustrations have long become part of the legal record as the visual documentation of a trial. In the United States, the tradition of creating courtroom sketches and their reproduction in newspapers dates back to the 19th century. Before the invention of photography, to help sell papers, engravings of courtroom drawings accompanied articles about the presiding judges, attorneys, petitioners and criminals. These images, at times caricatures, were made by courtroom artists commenting on social and political life and putting their artistic skills to commercial use. Newspapers sold better with illustrations offsetting blocks of text.

Due to insupportable disruptions that cameras would cause in courtrooms in the 20th century, the status of courtroom illustrations underwent little change. The debate for and against cameras in the courtroom has raged across jurisdictions for nearly a century. Most judges disallow cameras in their court for fear that they might interfere with the proceedings and could be used as an excuse to overturn a decision. To preserve decorum, even smartphones oftentimes must be checked with the guards. When courthouses are closed to cameras, and no photography is allowed, courtroom illustrators serve as a conduit from the public space to the public's eye. Their tools of the trade are discretely set up for quick deployment.

Everything is a judgment call: whether to allow cameras in the courtrooms or not, what to wear, what to say, where to sit, how to interpret reams of legal filings to tell tales of offense and defense? Courtroom illustrators also have to make decisions regarding which moments and compositions to memorialize. Their inspiration is coupled with stylistic and reporting instincts. Are courtroom illustrators able to be objective when they capture scenes and expressions? Do they have to be, all the while adding to the legal and visual historical record?

Courtroom illustrators reflect the human condition. For example, the illustrations created at the 5Pointz trial document both legal and art history in the making. People of all ages and types took an interest in the case concerned with mutilated street art at an abandoned industrial complex in Long Island, New York. Plaintiffs, more than two dozen artists, alleged violations of their intellectual property and the Visual Artists Rights Act. Artist after artist took the stand to explain their training, technique, and influences in creating the street art whitewashed by the defendant's real estate owner. The decision in favor of the artists, written by Judge Frederic Block of the Eastern District of New York, is accompanied by over 50 pages of art reproductions. The legal record

5POINTZ TRIAL ILLUSTRATION BY ELIZABETH WILLIAMS

DE SOLE V KNOEDLER ILLUSTRATION BY ELIZABETH WILLIAMS

of the trial is completed by Elizabeth Williams' drawings, which captured the colorful spectacle as it unfolded: the aged judge, the outraged defendant, the impassioned plaintiffs, the legal teams for both sides, the jury, and the public.

Another art law case, *DeSole v. Knoedler,* also received attention and a unique treatment from courtroom illustrators. It concerned the demise of the oldest privately owned art gallery in the United States. Gray haired plaintiffs, upright posture of one of the defendants, bold and bright stripes of the fake Rothko (the subject of the multi-million dollar dispute between aggrieved collectors and the gallery that sold them a fake)—all these images, an inextricable part of the legal history, as not one but two courtroom artists raced to capture witnesses on the stand, the demeanor of the named parties, and all the officers of the court working towards a resolution. While the case settled before a verdict, a trove of illustrations made by Elizabeth Williams and Victor Juhasz were reproduced by *Observer, Artforum, Artnews, The Art Newspaper,* and many other media outlets.

Blending artistic training with journalistic inquisitiveness, each courtroom illustrator sees and renders the case they attend in a uniquely personal way, with more or less humor, precision, flair. Some, like Richard Tomlinson prefer black-and-white line sketches (page 103). Others have a signature shading technique or are trained in making fashion drawings and thus place more emphasis on shading and the cut of suits. Others still capture the architectural almost aerial quality of the courtroom (page 241).

The moments in a courtroom captured by court artists enrich our immutable visual and historical record. Even if the legal outcomes change on appeal or through legislative efforts, portraits of those who have appeared before Lady Justice remain for the benefit of not only legal and historical record but also the imagination of art collectors, and so enter the realm of art trade. With *The Illustrated Courtroom: 50+ Years of Court Art,* now in its 2nd edition, courtroom art continues to gain momentum and recognition as a genre, worthy of collecting and study.

Irina Tarsis, Esq. is an art historian and a practicing commercial attorney specializing in art, cultural heritage and nonprofit governance legal issues. As the Founder and Director of the Center for Art Law, a New York-based nonprofit organization, she has extensive experience mentoring students in different arts-related fields, regarding art market issues, alternative dispute resolution and property rights. Tarsis publishes and consults on a range of issues including due diligence in the art trade, copyright infringement and fair use, artists' rights, restitution, authenticity and provenance research.

INTRODUCTION

This updated edition of *The Illustrated Courtroom* came to be because the world of court art has evolved so dramatically since our book's first edition. Trial art is now a fixture both in the 24/7 news cycle and in the fast-moving online world. And numerous epic news stories that broke in the past few years proved hard to ignore.

We welcomed the opportunity to include some notable examples. The #MeToo social movement exploded internationally in 2017, signaling massive support for victims of sexual assault. Uber-powerful Hollywood movie producer Harvey Weinstein's precipitous fall was at its heart, following decades of rumors of his sexually predatory behavior. In February 2020, I drew Weinstein being found guilty of rape and criminal sexual acts then sentenced to 23 years in prison.

Artist Aggie Kenny's work is also featured in this book. She and I covered multimillionaire financier Jeffrey Epstein's July 2019 arraignment on sex trafficking charges in New York. Epstein was first convicted as a sex offender back in 2008 but unlike in 2008, in 2019, he faced major prison time. However, on August 10, before he could stand trial, he was found dead in his cell. The story and theories on how Epstein died gripped the nation.

We court artists have always needed nerves of steel plus an aptitude for speed and precision, but now, with the Internet's meme culture, our work is ever more closely scrutinized. Any perceived failure to produce a good likeness of a famous face triggers a flood of criticism. In 2015, an artist's rendition of New England Patriots' football star Tom Brady at the #Deflategate proceedings—which followed allegations that Brady's team had cheated by using under-inflated balls—was pilloried as unflattering and unrecognizable. The illustration swiftly went viral. Its artist was heavily criticized as parodies and memes erupted, ridiculing her artwork.

The effect of the COVID-19 pandemic on the courts has been significant. Courtroom artists faced a whole new challenge, people's faces behind masks, behind barriers or on video. Limited seating in courtrooms due to social distancing. At the Britney Spears conservatorship, hearing some lawyers made their arguments via video, while others were in court wearing masks. Artists drew the R. Kelly sex trafficking trial from a blurry video feed piped into an overflow courtroom. These episodes alone are proof positive that we courtroom artists now inhabit a whole new world.

Elizabeth Williams

MEET THE ARTISTS

Four artists' work is presented in this book along with my own. First, if it was not for Emmy-nominee BILL ROBLES, I would not be a court artist. Without question, he's been the major influence on my career. I'd studied fashion and general illustration at Parsons School of Design and knew very little about court illustrations until, in 1979, I saw a show of Bill's work. His drawing, design, color and style were just exquisite. His artwork was marvelous and memorable. Meeting Bill in May, 1980, inspired me to pursue a career in the court art field and changed my life forever.

I met HOWARD BRODIE while covering the John DeLorean trial. He was tall and dressed head to toe in black, his signature color. He always was accessorized with opera glasses around his neck or perched above his glasses.

Watching him work close up, I was in awe of Howard's technique. He'd start by making one tiny mark on his paper then adding another and another. At first, I couldn't imagine what he was drawing but eventually a face came into focus, formed out of those tiny marks. It was as if he danced on the page with his pencil.

I first saw Emmy-winner AGGIE KENNY when she flew to L.A. from New York to cover the John DeLorean pre-trial hearing for ABC News. Aggie pretty much kept to herself. She gets so absorbed in her artwork she completely switches off the outside world. When Aggie gets into her zone, that's it.

Her watercolor and gouache technique—layering on the paint to produce rich, complex colors—was like nothing I'd ever seen. She is basically self-taught; a truly remarkable natural talent. She creates beautiful majestic courtroom scenes and marvelous portraits like no other.

RICHARD TOMLINSON'S bold artwork immediately captivated me when I first saw it. Richard won awards in many prestigious juried shows and had a stunning ability to draw and design simultaneously, working with remarkable skill, speed and passion. Richard never stopped drawing, be it a judge, a piece of evidence, a reporter or even a typewriter in the pressroom.

Bill, Howard, Aggie, Richard—four great reportage artists with distinct points of view and unique techniques. Their artwork is honest, direct and compelling because they put their hearts and souls into it. It's been an honor to be in the courtroom with them. This book, created with award-winning writer Sue Russell, is a labor of love. It fulfils my dream of preserving their stories, their work and this history.

Elizabeth Williams

PART I: THE ART OF LAW

INSIDE THE WORLD OF COURT ART
Great Expectations: Famous Faces

Inside the very best court artists are fine artists waiting to get out. However, crushing deadlines, said Elizabeth Williams, "can turn a potential master work into an ordinary one." The ticking clock gets even louder when trying to render a perfect likeness of a famous face. "Time always affects the quality of a finished drawing or likeness," said Bill Robles, "and what could have been a fabulous piece sometimes falls short."

Robles really nailed Michael Jackson's iconic features, though he was plagued by self-doubt throughout Jackson's trial: "Even though I am pretty confident, there is always the fear of not capturing a celebrity likeness. As one of my old Art Center instructors used to say, 'Thank God for erasers.'"

> "When someone's face is known all over the world, there's no faking it." —BILL ROBLES

Aggie Kenny described "definite electricity in the air when celebrities are in court." She found Mick Jagger memorable because "he was cracking jokes and appeared to be having a great time"—unusual among people in court.

The late Richard Tomlinson was determined never to be impressed by the famous. He feared being impressed might give him a mental block. His trick was to adjust his perception and see celebrated subjects "just as interesting shapes and not as real people."

> "If you don't quite capture them, there are thousands of critics on hand to let you know it." —AGGIE KENNY

Mick Jagger faced plagiarism charges in a White Plains, New York, courtroom in April 1988. Jamaican reggae singer Patrick Alley had sued for a share of the star's royalties from "Just Another Night," Jagger's number one hit from "She's the Boss," his 1985 debut solo album. Alley alleged Jagger stole his song of the same title, written several years earlier.

Jagger affably signed autographs during breaks. "But," said Williams, "when he took the witness stand, he was very ticked off. You don't usually see him looking grumpy. Capturing his emotions and expression was quite challenging, but I felt I got there in the end. The jurors seemed totally enraptured with him. It was a very unusual trial because the two songs were picked apart in great detail. Their tempos, keys, rhythms, structures, were all meticulously analyzed by music experts."

Jurors heard samplings of Jagger's and Alley's live and recorded music plus music experts' analysis. The judge instructed them that "accidental similarity is not actionable plagiarism." Their verdict vindicated Jagger.

ILLUSTRATION BY ELIZABETH WILLIAMS

ILLUSTRATION BY BILL ROBLES

PARIS HILTON

The Beverly Hills heiress's tiara toppled on May 4, 2007. After several run-ins with law enforcement and violating her three years' probation for an earlier alcohol-related traffic conviction, she appeared before Los Angeles Superior Court Judge Michael T. Sauer. The socialite/reality TV star had been arrested three times for driving on a suspended license and stopped once for recklessly driving her Bentley without headlights after dark.

She cavalierly arrived for her sentencing twenty minutes late. Bill Robles observed that she was "fully composed on the witness stand and totally confident as she testified."

However, Judge Sauer was unpersuaded by Ms. Hilton's claims that she did not realize her license was suspended and granted the prosecutor's request to revoke her bail. When he sentenced her to 45 days in a cell, Robles recalled, she was horrified and distraught.

Ms. Hilton's sentence became fodder for late night television, leading Jay Leno to quip: "A lot of people were upset about this. They wanted the death penalty."

ILLUSTRATION BY ELIZABETH WILLIAMS

TEKASHI 6ix9ine

Brooklyn rapper Tekashi 6ix9ine's garish rainbow-colored hair was gone. But, with his signature proliferation of tattoos, Tekashi69, aka Daniel Hernandez, was still a fun subject for Elizabeth Williams to draw on the witness stand in 2019. The visual antithesis of so many defendants' bland business style, "He was like a tattooed fashion model," she noted. "It's not only his face. He has 6s and 9s all over his fingers and arms. Thank goodness for binoculars!"

Tekashi69, then 23, faced racketeering and conspiracy murder charges which could have earned him at least 37 years in prison. Williams drew him as he testified for the government—the prosecution's star witness at the trial of two former gang member cronies from the violent Nine Trey Gangsta Bloods.

"Tekashi was really disarming," she recalled. "He was charismatic, animated and remarkably articulate. He leaned over to speak into the microphone, clearly aware of its importance."

In December 2019, District Judge Paul Engelmayer acknowledged his bravery in testifying but still sentenced him to two years. "You," he said, "essentially joined Murder Incorporated."

ILLUSTRATION BY AGGIE KENNY

WOODY ALLEN

In March 1993, Aggie Kenny was parachuted in to cover the bitter, ongoing, custody battle being waged in Manhattan Supreme Court by director Woody Allen against actress Mia Farrow, his former partner of 12 years. Kenny found it "a challenge to suddenly have to get a likeness of these two famous people."

Farrow had 14 biological and adopted children. After their relationship ended, Allen sought custody of his three in the mix: son Satchel (now Ronan), 5, plus their co-adoptive children, son Moses and daughter Dylan.

Trouble flared in January 1992 when Mia found nude photographs Allen had taken of Mia's adoptive daughter Soon-Yi Previn, some 35 years his junior, and discovered their affair. That August, Dylan, then 7, complained that Allen had sexually assaulted her. Allen has always flatly denied this, describing Farrow as a vindictive, scorned woman who had coached the child. Still, Acting Justice Elliott Wilk was unpersuaded. He ended Allen's visitation with Dylan until further review and on June 7, 1993, awarded Farrow custody of the trio.

ILLUSTRATION BY ELIZABETH WILLIAMS

TOM BRADY

The football world scandal #DeflateGate followed New England Patriots superstar quarterback, Tom Brady, and team staff being accused by the NFL (National Football League) of cheating their way to victory against the Indianapolis Colts. They were accused of deflating eleven of twelve footballs in January 2015's American Football Conference championship.

The league suspended Brady without pay for four games and fined the team $1 million. That summer, with the backing of the NFL Players Association, Brady went up against the NFL in federal court in New York, challenging his suspension.

Elizabeth Williams was not familiar with Brady, "but when he walked into court for his first settlement hearing, I was very pleased to see his perfect, male model features. For me, he was great to draw."

Judge Richard M. Berman nullified Brady's ban, allowing him back on the field. In April 2016, however, the U.S. Second Circuit Court of Appeals reinstated the suspension. Ultimately, Brady dropped his appeal efforts and accepted his fate.

The 45th U.S. president's now world-famous looming figure and trademark swagger were, like his blond hair, bushy eyebrows and pursed mouth, already evident in 1986 when Elizabeth Williams drew him in court. Then the owner of the New Jersey Generals team, he was the driving force in the United States Football League's (USFL's) antitrust case against the mighty National Football League (NFL) and NFL commissioner Pete Rozelle. The plaintiffs alleged that the elite NFL had cramped its style by establishing a monopoly in television broadcasting rights.

In court, Williams observed, the jury seemed very star struck by the 40-year-old property developer as opposed to seemingly stodgier NFL characters like Commissioner Pete Rozelle.

"Trump was in court a lot and was clearly very interested in the case," she recalled. "My only direct interaction with Trump was once when I entered the courthouse in a hurry and rushed into the elevator looking down. When I looked up, his imposing form was standing right there. It took me aback. I immediately turned around and pushed the button to exit the elevator. I like to keep my distance from my subjects so it was a little awkward. One good thing about Trump, however, is that he didn't mind being drawn."

Harvey Meyerson, the Generals' and USFL's lawyer, was a bombastic little man with a pinkie ring and a Rolls Royce who was later disbarred for overcharging clients.

"At the trial, they were quite a team," Williams recalled. "The large, imposing figure of Trump and stocky little Harvey Meyerson. During Meyerson's summation, he used a pointer, banging it loudly on a desk, yelling and carrying on. It was quite a show. But all eyes were on Trump, especially during jury deliberations. He hung around and chatted with reporters and with his legal team."

The jury found that the NFL did indeed have a monopoly and held it liable for one antitrust violation. It awarded the USFL one dollar. A resounding defeat for Trump and the apparent end of the USFL.

ILLUSTRATION BY ELIZABETH WILLIAMS

Freeze the Moment

Court artists are always primed for action. They live in a perpetual state of readiness—ready to recognize and illustrate pivotal, unexpected and interesting scenes the second they unfold. Ready to freeze the moment. As Richard Tomlinson put it, "There may be some time to consider how best to lay out a picture—or none. You never know what is going to happen."

Frequently, hours of waiting around precede crushing deadlines. Suddenly the artists must work at a feverish pace, powered by adrenaline and coffee. They can't miss. And there are no excuses. Reputations stand or fall on results.

LATE ARTIST HOWARD BRODIE DRAWN BY THE LATE RICHARD TOMLINSON, *THE RICHARD TOMLINSON COURTROOM DRAWINGS COLLECTION*, JOHN JAY COLLEGE OF CRIMINAL JUSTICE

By definition, court artists go where cameras can't. They bring trials and arraignments and sentencing hearings to life for those not in court. They create the only visual record. And they cover everything, said Bill Robles, "from celebrities, spies, terrorists, corporate corruption, political scandals, killers, mass murderers, celebrity custody hearings, to sex scandals, child molestation cases and military court marshals."

Every courtroom is different. Artists drink in the broad sweep, the atmosphere, the cast of characters, plus telling details. They are keen observers of the subtle and overt. A glance, a clenched fist, a tear on a cheek, a tightened facial muscle, posture, mannerisms, prominent features, sartorial style (or lack thereof), colors, distinctive personalities, plus any sudden, explosive or news-making moves.

"Sometimes, with a case like Watergate, you know you're watching history," said Kenny. "Often you don't really have that sense. And it's probably just as well because you might approach it differently."

> "When Chuck Jones drew his marvelous Bugs Bunny cartoons, it's doubtful he foresaw them achieving their current iconic status. Similarly, I doubt those who hired us to cover important trials realized that they were creating a wealth of historic visual documents." —ELIZABETH WILLIAMS

It's demanding work. "When everyone else takes a lunch, coffee or bathroom break," said Williams, "we often have to work right through." Robles has added finishing touches to his work in a moving car, in an airplane and in a California governor's waiting room. Robles contended that any artist who doesn't relish or thrive on pressure is in the wrong business.

The early bird catches the most coveted seat and artists jockey for good viewing angles. A tiny edge in seat allocation can really count, so artists sometimes arrive before dawn and wait outside in rain or snow. By the time Williams took her seat at the Martha Stewart trial, her fingers felt so frozen she was afraid they wouldn't defrost in time to work.

> "Sometimes I feel like a duck hunter waiting in a bush, waiting for that turn of the head, that glance, that show of emotion. I sit and stare, then move lightning fast."
> —ELIZABETH WILLIAMS

Reporters need only to hear testimony to do their jobs, but artists must see it. "We are usually allowed to sit in the front row and sometimes even the jury box," said Williams. "I look for a vantage point where I can see all the key characters in a well-composed shot and show as much of the courtroom as possible, just as a photographer would."

The judicious use of opera glasses can be a lifesaver when artists work at a distance. Howard Brodie and Richard Tomlinson routinely used them to zoom in on their subjects. Tomlinson would have preferred to be invisible, but sometimes had no choice. "I'm sure my presence intimidated my subjects," he said. "They had no way to hide."

THE LATE RICHARD TOMLINSON DRAWN BY AGGIE KENNY

"The more discreet you are, the more you can work unseen, the better. People who aren't aware of you don't pose or change their expressions or turn their heads."
—RICHARD TOMLINSON

At disgraced college football coach Jerry Sandusky's child molestation trial, Aggie Kenny was seated "a mile away and the lighting was poor. I relied on binoculars to see what the man looked like."

Mishaps are rare, but they happen. For years, Kenny traveled extensively under contract to ABC and CBS; her most memorable red-face moment was in a Miami courtroom while heavily pregnant, when she sat down on a bench already overloaded with reporters. "I upended the thing, along with all the reporters on it," she sighed. "Everyone was very polite. Basically, the judge and lawyers carried on as if nothing had happened so they wouldn't embarrass me. But I still cringe when I think about it."

Williams spilled indelible ink on the Los Angeles Federal Courthouse's rather pristine-looking carpet. Mortified, she never used ink in court again.

Courtrooms are somber places, often awash with the palpable pain, grief and anger of violent crime victims and victims' friends and loved ones. But artists are too busy to get caught up in their emotions. It wouldn't be professional to let their personal feelings show. As Tomlinson—who liked a little levity—once quipped, he only fought back tears in court "if a court officer or big attorney was blocking my view and I couldn't move to a better angle and had less than three minutes to make the drawing."

For court artists, preparation is all. Tomlinson's philosophy was never to "go out the door without checking your art supplies 10 times over." Once, as Kenny raced from the Washington air shuttle en route to a job, "I grabbed a portfolio from the bulkhead thinking it was mine. It wasn't, as I discovered after arriving at court. I had time to race off to a store to purchase very primitive materials. It was the closest real-time situation to my most persistent anxiety dreams, which include things like finding moats around courtrooms, having an empty portfolio and being caught without a pen."

> "Who was the greatest face for me to draw? The next one."
> —HOWARD BRODIE

Ultimately, each courtroom's personality is a reflection of the presiding judge. And some jurists rule with an iron fist. "Sometimes, they issue ominous warnings," said Kenny, "about what will happen if something displeases them like the sound of an errant cell phone, of scratching pastels or of any conversation."

One persnickety judge even groused that Howard Brodie's bald head was distracting. "I considered buying a wig and charging it to CBS!" Brodie said later. Welcome to the world of court art.

Beauty and the Beard

Distinctive features like a beard, a pronounced nose or even accessories like glasses or clothing give artists an obvious visual handle. "When I see a witness or defendant with a terrific full beard like film director Francis Ford Coppola, who is also a wonderfully high-spirited individual and a huge presence, I can't believe my luck," Robles observed. "I think, 'Wow! I get paid to do this!'"

A pretty face can be a delight for some artists while others find symmetry and beauty more challenging. Most artists agree that it is difficult to capture a good likeness of a bland, nondescript visage. Williams faced that challenge at the hearings of Donald Trump's attorney Michael Cohen, drawing the blonde porn star Stormy Daniels versus the flaccid face of Cohen. Williams recalled, "Daniels was a breeze, Cohen's face drove me nuts. It would have helped if he had facial hair or even glasses. There was nothing."

> "The comments we get from our subjects range from compliments to criticisms about having given someone insufficient hair or too many chins." —AGGIE KENNY

Equally Kenny loves the idiosyncratic. "I love having my attention drawn immediately to the quirky or unusual in court," she says. "It provides a foil in an otherwise dull and predictable setting. An interesting design element like a hat or dark sunglasses on a heavy-set mob witness can be the foundation of a composition."

FRANCIS FORD COPPOLA

To Robles, movie director Francis Ford Coppola's beard was a visual godsend in a 1984 civil court case in Los Angeles centered on the movie "The Cotton Club," set in the famed 1920s nightclub. The case pitted famed Hollywood producer Robert Evans against the film's primary investors, Las Vegas casino owners Edward and Fred Doumani, and Coppola, its distressed director.

Evans sued the Doumanis, who countersued for control of the project. And Coppola's testimony bolstered their claim that with Evans at the helm, the film was in disarray. "My only desire is to get out of this job and get on with my life," Coppola told the court. "He was visibly upset," Robles recalled. U.S. District Court Judge Irving Hill gave Evans control of the production and a relieved Coppola creative control.

MICHAEL COHEN & STORMY DANIELS:
The Dirty Fixster and the Porn Star

April 16, 2018, found Donald Trump's longtime attorney, confidant and fixer, in court trying to block federal prosecutors from reviewing more than 4 million electronic and paper documents the FBI seized in raids on his home, hotel room and office. Citing attorney-client privilege, Cohen, then under investigation for crimes like tax evasion and campaign finance violations, sought a temporary restraining order to keep them sealed.

With various legal eagles facing off in court, the fireworks began. Stormy Daniels, whom Cohen paid $130,000 to buy her silence about her alleged 2006 sexual affair with Trump, also had an interest in Cohen's seized files. She was suing Trump and Cohen to void the non-disclosure agreement she claimed Cohen forced her to sign in return for her payment.

"We'd heard rumors that Stormy Daniels was coming that day," Elizabeth Williams recalled, "but I was getting anxious because she was late. Fortunately, she arrived just before the hearing started and sat where we could see her!

"Importantly for me, she was visually striking with her lavender jacket and bright blonde hair and fun to draw. A perfect Trump type of woman. Cohen was tough with his nondescript, flaccid cheeks and round eyes.

"Daniels appeared almost bored throughout what was a lively, if lengthy, hearing. I found it all very interesting anyway, because you could tell Cohen truly was in hot water. He was almost defiant the first day—until Stormy appeared when he almost looked sheepish, like a kid caught pulling a little girl's pigtails."

By August 21st, Cohen was back in court pleading guilty to eight criminal charges and "he was an emotional mess." Cohen claimed the Trump organization reimbursed him for Daniels' hush money during the run-up to Trump's 2016 election when revelations of affairs might have damaged his presidential campaign. Cohen said he made the payment at Trump's direction, "for the principal purpose of influencing the election."

Cohen wore his emotional rollercoaster ride on his face. "His moods and expressions were constantly in flux," said Williams. "I thought I would lose my mind trying to get a good likeness. I kept starting drawings then, not satisfied, starting over. It was a true exercise in frustration. Later, I realized I had made seventeen false starts!"

On December 12, District Court Judge William H. Pauley III sentenced Cohen, then 52, to three years in prison for what he called "a veritable smorgasbord" of criminal conduct.

Stormy Daniels seated behind Michael Cohen in court.
ILLUSTRATION BY ELIZABETH WILLIAMS

JOAQUIN "EL CHAPO" GUZMÁN & WIFE EMMA CORONEL AISPURO: The Drug Lord & His Lady

Mexican and American authorities spent years toppling El Chapo, the ruthless drug trafficking kingpin, head of Mexico's infamous Sinaloa Cartel. In January 2017, El Chapo was extradited to the US to face seventeen charges including heading a multi-billion dollar narcotics trafficking enterprise, money laundering and conspiracy to commit murder.

Notorious for his brazen escapes via underground tunnels (one a nearly mile-long passageway from his Mexican prison cell's shower), El Chapo presented a major security risk. The Brooklyn federal courthouse was on high alert.

During the trial, starting at 3 a.m., Elizabeth Williams lined up outside the courthouse along with the throngs of press, all braving the cold, winter weather to secure their precious seats. Photographs of 5′6″ El Chapo ("Shorty") had not prepared her for so undistinguished and diminutive a man.

"Whenever I trained my binoculars on him to get a better view, he'd stare straight back at me with this unnerving, hard gaze," she recalled. "But there was nothing to grasp visually, beyond the moustache which he grew later before sentencing. He frequently stared into the public seats to look at, or look for, his wife, Emma Coronel Aispuro. She was a constant presence and loyal supporter."

When they wed in 2007, Aispuro was in her teens, he a fugitive in his fifties. Williams loved Mrs. El Chapo's "perfect fashion face, Barbie Doll, hourglass figure and shiny dark hair. With her clearly defined sense of style, she appealed to my lifelong passion for fashion. I analyzed faces like hers while studying fashion illustration. She had her own fashion line. I loved that she brought glamour to such a challenging and difficult trial."

On February 12, 2019, El Chapo was found guilty on all counts. His wife heard the verdict in Spanish over her headphones. Further escape notwithstanding, the Guzmáns' life together was over. But El Chapo blew his wife a kiss and the couple exchanged a thumbs up.

He was back in court in July for sentencing. Fascinated court watchers slept outside the courthouse overnight. Judge Brian M. Cogan sentenced El Chapo to life in prison plus thirty years without the possibility of parole and $12.6 billion in fines.

Emma Coronel Aispuro will forego her trademark designer duds for a matching prison jumpsuit during a long stay behind bars. Believed to be a cartel go-between for her husband, his sons and associates, she was arrested in February 2021, tried and convicted. That November, she was sentenced to three years in prison.

Joaquin Guzman ("El Chapo") making a statement during his sentencing via interpreter on July 17, 2019. Below, Emma Coronel Aispuro, wife of "El Chapo" seated during trial in 2019.
ILLUSTRATION BY ELIZABETH WILLIAMS

CHARCOAL AND CAMERAS:
Playing by the Rules of Law

Cameras are nearly universally banned in federal courts. And they're completely banned in the U.S. Supreme Court. In 1996, Justice David H. Souter proclaimed that "the day you see a camera come into our courtroom, it's going to roll over my dead body."

Beyond that, cameras are permitted in state courtrooms in all 50 states. But a mix of rules, restrictions and judicial discretion ultimately governs precisely which court hearings and trials are photographed. Today 36 states allow television cameras in their trial courts; still more allow them at the appellate level. But some states prohibit photographing sexual assault victims, juveniles, witnesses or jurors.

> "The holy grail of cameras in courts is the federal court. Once they have free access there, we artists are gone, gone, gone."
> —ELIZABETH WILLIAMS

When cameras are excluded from high-profile trials, you can count on television networks' and news organizations' attorneys to fight for access. But that is not to say that they don't value—and sometimes count on—artists' contributions. Court art has a long and storied history. Political satirists produced it in England 300 years ago. And demand for court art grew fast in the 1960s— right alongside television news' appetite for images.

In the 1990s, the media circus around O.J. Simpson's murder trial, which aired almost gavel-to-gavel on the Court TV channel, led many judges to question the merits of cameras in courtrooms. Over the years, however, the trend has continued in many states toward allowing more use of cameras during court proceedings.

Tomlinson often drew courtroom scenes while waiting for the proceedings to begin. ILLUSTRATION BY RICHARD TOM-LINSON, *THE RICHARD TOMLINSON COURTROOM DRAWINGS COLLECTION*, JOHN JAY COLLEGE OF CRIMINAL JUSTICE

Artful Dodgers

Unlike photographers, artists typically aren't required to make formal requests for permission to work in courtrooms. But judges sometimes still issue edicts about what is off limits. They are very protective of minors and alleged sex crimes victims, and news editors also often naturally lean towards discretion. It's a huge change from the 1980s, with its rash of trials related to sexual abuse at daycare centers.

"We recall being allowed to draw a victim as young as four years old," said Williams. "In 1985, we even drew children who sucked their thumbs while testifying about sexual abuse. That seems shocking now."

> "I've hidden children's faces behind microphones. You try to
> be creative about keeping to the rules." —BILL ROBLES

In 2012, the victim protection issue arose in Bellefonte, Pennsylvania, in the child molestation trial of former Penn State football coach Jerry Sandusky. Sandusky, 68, faced 52 counts of child sex abuse involving 10 boys spanning a period of more than 15 years. Aggie Kenny asked for guidelines and adhered to Judge John Cleland's mandate that illustrations not be exact likenesses. Sandusky was convicted and sentenced to 30 to 60 years. "Victim #4 is not even a good likeness, let alone exact," she said. "But his white shirt, khakis and polite demeanor conveyed a good sense of his presence without giving anything away. But my success in rendering a bad likeness was immaterial to my client because, of its own volition, the Associated Press made the editorial decision to remove both depictions of victim #4 from the illustration completely."

"Judges often instruct us not to show any facial detail to protect jurors' and witnesses' anonymity," said Williams. These days, showing jurors' faces is generally restricted on high-profile cases.

> "I employ all sorts of tricks when I can't draw someone's face. If
> they hide their faces by holding up a hand or leaning forward
> in their chairs, I go for it and draw." —ELIZABETH WILLIAMS

Williams couldn't show the jurors at financier Rajat Gupta's insider trading trial in 2012. She likes to meet such challenges creatively and subtly. By sitting way off to the side, for example, she only sees the backs of jurors' heads or catches really extreme, unidentifiable profiles:

"Ideally, I don't want it to look as if I am avoiding drawing people's faces. Witnesses typically look towards the lawyer asking the questions, but witness Anil Kumar was very focused on engaging with the jury. Perhaps he was avoiding looking at Gupta because he was uncomfortable testifying against his old friend and mentor. But the jurors turned their heads towards Kumar, presenting me with a great angle to conceal their faces in a natural way."

Williams hid the jurors' faces while Anil Kumar, former director of the global financial consulting firm McKinsey, testified as a witness at financier Rajat Gupta's insider trading trial in New York in June 2012. After entering a guilty plea to charges of insider trading in 2010, Kumar went on to become a powerful prosecution witness in the trials of Gupta and Raj Rajaratnam. ILLUSTRATION: ELIZABETH WILLIAMS/BLOOMBERG NEWS

Former Penn State football coach Jerry Sandusky in court with now-adult victim #4 on the witness stand. Artist Aggie Kenny's rendering of him was not a good likeness, per the judge's request. Her illustration of a large photographic image of victim #4 as a boy—fleetingly projected for the jurors to see—was a super-vague impression and non-identifiable. Nevertheless, her client, the Associated Press, removed both. Also memorable at Sandusky's trial: his casual hands-in-pockets stance when he was being sentenced to 30-60 years. "I have never ever seen a defendant do that," said Williams. "His sneering demeanor throughout was inescapable," Kenny agreed. "To me, he exuded the sense that he somehow thought himself above it all." ILLUSTRATION BY AGGIE KENNY

Photographer and Artist:
An Uneasy Alliance

News editors work at warp speed with photographers, so their expectations for artists can sometimes be unrealistic. "There can be a lot of anxiety if they don't have your artwork in hand instantaneously," said Kenny, "which of course they don't." News editors covered all the bases in the Dominique Strauss-Kahn case, an international headline-grabber, by assigning both artists and photographers. Before charges against him were eventually dropped, the former International Monetary Fund chief was charged with sexually assaulting a Manhattan hotel maid.

Elizabeth Williams drew Dominique Strauss-Kahn, who faced sexual assault charges, at his bail hearing on May 19, 2011. Bail was denied but was eventually granted. The criminal charges were dismissed six weeks later after prosecutors lost faith in the alleged victim's credibility. Left to right: Assistant District Attorney Artie McConnell, Strauss-Kahn's wife, Anne Sinclair, and daughter, Camille Strauss-Kahn, defense lawyer William Taylor (standing) and Strauss-Kahn, looking over his shoulder. ILLUSTRATION: ELIZABETH WILLIAMS/CNBC NEWS

Strauss-Kahn, whose then-wife was French television star/heiress Anne Sinclair, spent only a few days in custody before being released under luxurious house arrest. But Williams saw him perched on a bench alongside accused drug dealers and small-time crooks—with no photographers around. "I had my radar up for something different," she notes. "And that little scene to me spoke volumes."

"We're a necessary evil. Networks would rather have cameras, but if there's no camera, you're it." —BILL ROBLES

Often, photographers don't have permission to shoot in court. That was the case when Strauss-Kahn's wife Anne and daughter Camille showed up. Mother and daughter were holding hands.

"It was an emotional moment we all wanted to capture," said Williams. "Strauss-Kahn looked back at his wife and daughter, trying to catch their eyes, clearly seeking some kind of acknowledgment. His daughter looked his way and smiled. But tellingly, his wife—looking somewhere between seething and traumatized—stared straight ahead. I got the moment."

"There can be expectations that you should work as fast as a digital camera." —AGGIE KENNY

KEEPING COURT ART JOURNALISTICALLY PURE

We feel strongly about the integrity of our journalistic method. As we are artists with distinctive styles observing constant courtroom activity, some subjectivity is inevitable. However, we applaud the Associated Press Guidelines. They are the gold standard and show that top news organizations hold courtroom art to the same standards journalistically as photo journalism. Which is just as it should be.

—AGGIE KENNY, BILL ROBLES AND ELIZABETH WILLIAMS

AP'S COURTROOM ARTISTRY GUIDELINES

Understanding that drawing as an artistic medium is different in many ways from photography, the Associated Press must still insist that basic rules of image integrity and truthfulness be adhered to in the creation of courtroom sketches, drawings or paintings.

Designed to ensure its images always tell the truth, AP's policy on handling photographic images prohibits electronic image manipulation with Photoshop, for example. AP requires court art to "be as faithful and truthful a rendering of the scene as possible, without embellishments of content or timelines that could misrepresent the actual sequence of events depicted." A sampling from the AP Guidelines:

- Individuals and objects must be pictured as they were in the courtroom.
- Spatial relationships of objects and figures (judges and defendants, for example) should be rendered accurately. If the distance between subjects is not aesthetically pleasing or makes for awkward compositions, then separate close up drawings of the protagonists may be preferable.
- Finally, no artistic license should be taken with regard to facial expressions or personal characteristics of subjects.

PART II: SENSATIONAL TRIALS

JACK RUBY: *A Shot Too Far*

Jack Ruby executed Lee Harvey Oswald—who was handcuffed to homicide detective James Leavelle while being transported between jails—on national television 48 hours after the assassination of President John F. Kennedy on November 22, 1963. Ruby jumped out from a crowd of reporters in the basement of Dallas police headquarters and fired a single fatal shot into Oswald's torso.

Ruby, 52, a portly, balding, limelight-loving nightclub owner, had been mingling with *Dallas Morning News* staffers. Ruby, who grew up in poverty in Chicago, aspired to status and class. He wanted to be revered or idolized and loved schmoozing with cops and being in the thick of the media frenzy.

Artist Howard Brodie was at home in Palo Alto, California, when he heard the devastating news about the president. He'd drawn Kennedy's and Richard Nixon's portraits for *Newsweek* covers during the 1960 presidential campaign. Learning that cameras would not be allowed in court during Ruby's trial, he took action.

"I called an old World War II buddy who was a CBS executive. 'How're you going to cover it?' I said. 'I don't know,' he said. 'Do you want to do it?'"

With that, Brodie had landed his first criminal trial assignment for television news. "I flew to Dallas to draw the assassin of the assassin of President Kennedy," Brodie recalled. "As I got settled in the courtroom, Jack Ruby sat near the rail chatting with the press."

Jury selection began on February 17, 1964, in Dallas Criminal Court, very close to where the president died. Reporters descended from all over the world, and the judge moved to a larger 194-seat courtroom. "One by one," said Brodie, "prospective jurors on the witness stand were asked if they could sentence Jack to death, facing him a few feet away. Many couldn't."

Personal injury lawyer Melvin Belli led Ruby's defense pro bono. It was his first major criminal case. While Belli's predecessor was considering trying for a plea bargain, Belli had a more exotic—and risky—defense. He claimed that Ruby had a condition called psychomotor epilepsy that made him black out and rendered him momentarily insane when he shot Oswald.

The controversial San Francisco attorney struck Brodie as emotional and flamboyant. ("I'm not flamboyant, I'm colorful," Belli would say.) He was often visually startling and made dramatic entrances into court. He was sophisticated, silken-voiced and well-groomed with a neat bouffant hairstyle.

The Dallas courtroom where in 1964 Jack Ruby stood trial for shooting to death President Kennedy's alleged assassin, Lee Harvey Oswald. Left to right: Jack Ruby (sitting), his defense attorneys Melvin Belli (standing) and Joe H. Tonahill (sitting). Judge Joe Brown presiding. ILLUSTRATION: HOWARD BRODIE © ESTATE OF HOWARD BRODIE; IMAGE COURTESY OF THE LIBRARY OF CONGRESS, PRINTS & PHOTOGRAPHS DIVISION

Jack Ruby, killer of President John F. Kennedy's alleged assassin, Lee Harvey Oswald, was arraigned in the Dallas County Criminal Courthouse on March 4, 1964. Ruby (left), district attorney Henry Wade (center) and Ruby's chief defense attorney Melvin Belli (right). ILLUSTRATION: HOWARD BRODIE. © ESTATE OF HOWARD BRODIE; IMAGE COURTESY OF THE LIBRARY OF CONGRESS, PRINTS & PHOTOGRAPHS DIVISION

Belli carried a red velvet carpet bag as a briefcase and sometimes wore a cape. "He swept in, the inner folds of his dark coat aglow with red lining," said Brodie. A more conservative mood likely meant a black cashmere coat atop one of his Savile Row red-silk-lined suits. But he also wore sharp vests adorned with a fob watch, a red cummerbund and Byronesque flowing ties. And his high-heeled ankle boots—Congress gaiters—were doubtless another affront to cowboy-booted locals' sensibilities.

> "He (Belli) was a very pompous little bastard . . . He had the
> utmost contempt for us, and he and I didn't hit it off at all."
> —ASST. DISTRICT ATTORNEY WILLIAM F. ALEXANDER, WHO RETALIATED
> BY ADDRESSING BELLI AS "MR. BELLY"

Melvin Belli defended Jack Ruby, who assassinated Lee Harvey Oswald on camera, with gusto. Belli's animated, take-no-prisoners style became legendary. He pointed—and shouted—at attorneys, witnesses and the judge during the trial. ILLUSTRATIONS: HOWARD BRODIE © ESTATE OF HOWARD BRODIE; IMAGE COURTESY OF THE LIBRARY OF CONGRESS, PRINTS & PHOTOGRAPHS DIVISION

"The judge, sitting on an inflated rubber-doughnut cushion," said Brodie, "decreed that only those within the rail could smoke, denying newsmen and spectators the privilege."

But civility had its limits. During recesses, reporters vaulted the railing and clustered around the attorneys. They swarmed in again at day's end.

The trial began on March 4 with Belli's third wife looking on. Two days later, a drama unfolded with witness Karen Bennett Carlin—exotic dancer "Little Lynn"—who was due to give birth at any moment. Mrs. Belli and a female sheriff's deputy were escorting her to a restroom just as seven escapees from the building's sixth floor cells rushed through the courtroom hallways right past the Ruby trial.

Ruby looking at movie 3/5/64
showing Oswald

On March 5, 1964, murder defendant Jack Ruby and his jury watched the news footage that showed him shooting Lee Harvey Oswald. ILLUSTRATION: HOWARD BRODIE © ESTATE OF HOWARD BRODIE; IMAGE COURTESY OF THE LIBRARY OF CONGRESS, PRINTS & PHOTOGRAPHS DIVISION

Brandishing a realistic-looking fake gun fashioned from soap and painted black, Clarence D. Gregory grabbed Judge Mead's clerk, Mrs. Ruth Thornton. He tried to hide behind her to make his escape. Reportedly, "Little Lynn" was so terrified she shouted "He's after me! He's after me!" before she slumped to the floor and had to be revived.

Four prisoners were quickly recaptured and "Little Lynn" went on to take the stand. She said she spoke to Jack Ruby by telephone that Sunday and that he'd wired her money minutes before gunning down Oswald.

Police officer James Leavelle, who was handcuffed to Oswald that morning, testified that after shooting Oswald, Ruby shouted: "I hope the son of a bitch dies!"

"'I wanted to be a hero.'" —POLICE OFFICER JAMES LEAVELLE
REPORTING JACK RUBY'S WORDS ABOUT WHY HE KILLED OSWALD

Karen "Little Lynn" Bennett Carlin, a heavily pregnant exotic dancer who worked at Ruby's Carousel Club in Dallas. She took the witness stand at his trial on March 6, 1964. Earlier, Bennett was shaken when prisoners escaped the building's jail cells and pointed a fake gun at a court clerk. ILLUSTRATION: HOWARD BRODIE © ESTATE OF HOWARD BRODIE; IMAGE COURTESY OF THE LIBRARY OF CONGRESS, PRINTS & PHOTOGRAPHS DIVISION

Melvin Belli was known to like a drink or two and on March 11, Brodie noted on his illustration: "During day, Belli said he (Belli) wasn't feeling well. Jack Daniels and duck feathers."

Two days later, Belli put on his final witness, Dr. Frederic Gibbs, the pioneer of electroencephalographs (EEGs)—brain wave tests—and their analysis. But Dr. Gibbs surely disappointed Belli. He couldn't form an opinion on whether Ruby knew right from wrong.

The prosecutor said in his closing argument that "American justice is on trial. He thought he could kill Lee Oswald and become a hero."

Summations were wrapped up at 12:50 a.m. and the sequestered jurors grabbed some sleep, reconvening at 9 a.m. to determine Ruby's fate. Exactly 139 minutes later, they had a verdict. Judge Brown let cameras into the courtroom for the reading and once again, pandemonium ensued.

Ruby was found guilty of murder with malice and sentenced to death in the electric chair.

ADAMS APPLE
QUIVERED - HE
GULPED JUST BEFORE SENTENCE

Howard Brodie
3/14/64

RUBY — JUST BEFORE
VERDICT WAS READ

Verdict day: March 14, 1964. Trained to observe every little detail, Howard Brodie noticed Jack Ruby's Adam's apple quivering as he waited to hear his fate. ILLUSTRATION: HOWARD BRODIE © ESTATE OF HOWARD BRODIE; IMAGE COURTESY OF THE LIBRARY OF CONGRESS, PRINTS & PHOTOGRAPHS DIVISION

"Just before the panel brought in a death sentence, Ruby's
Adam's apple quivered and he gulped." —ARTIST HOWARD BRODIE

"You must pick up little details," Brodie explained. "And I always had to be objective. I couldn't have preconceived attitudes. I viewed the defendant as just another human being, and I simply drew what I saw."

Looking back at the television news footage of the Ruby verdict being read, Elizabeth Williams found it riveting to see Brodie in court, working under pressure: "It was probably not more than a minute or two, yet he captured Ruby's mood and his fear. Do you know how amazing that is?"

"Belli softly thanked the jurors," Brodie said, "then shouted, 'For a victory of bigotry and injustice!' A spectator turned to me and said, 'Did you ever see a lawyer act like this after losing a case?' I reminded her that a man's life, not a case, was lost."

Leaving court, Belli's rage continued to spill over as he called the trial "the greatest railroading kangaroo court disgrace in the history of American law . . ." Ruby's conviction was overturned in 1966, but he died before the new trial.

"I just wonder when these people (jurors) go to church tomorrow and take the Communion cup, whether it shouldn't curdle on their lips." —JACK RUBY'S ATTORNEY MELVIN BELLI AFTER THE VERDICT

Jack Ruby's chief defense attorney Melvin Belli held court with a scrum of reporters and cameras. ILLUSTRATION: HOWARD BRODIE © ESTATE OF HOWARD BRODIE; IMAGE COURTESY OF THE LIBRARY OF CONGRESS, PRINTS & PHOTOGRAPHS DIVISION

THE BLACK PANTHER 21: *Fear Rising*

Inside the New York State Supreme Court on February 2, 1970, Richard Tomlinson's first court art assignment, the New York Panther 21 case, was a landmark in an era of civil unrest. The news was full of revolutionaries, the air thick with violence.

The militant Black Panther Party (BPP) was founded in Oakland, California, in 1966 with goals as disparate as meals for schoolchildren and overthrowing the white power structure. The party's snarling panther emblem and signature uniform of black berets, black leather jackets and black pants (sometimes accessorized with weapons) were enough to intimidate, scare and enrage many Americans. Panther chapters sprang up nationwide and J. Edgar Hoover pronounced them the FBI's primary target and "the greatest threat to the internal security of the country."

The New York Panther 21 defendants were accused of conspiring to kill police officers and to use explosives to blow up railway lines, police stations, the Bronx Botanical Gardens and top Manhattan department stores. They faced charges of attempted murder, arson and possession of weapons, bomb-making materials and explosives.

> "Why would the Black Panther Party bomb the stores that people shop in?" —BLACK PANTHER PARTY MEMBER AFENI SHAKUR, FEBRUARY 1970

Their supporters were sure the 21 were framed. And their defense attorneys claimed that weapons and explosives in evidence were seized illegally.

The Panthers often struck Tomlinson, working for New York's Channel 5 WNEW News, as sullen and mean-looking, yet somehow more broken-down than terrifying. Since their arrests in pre-dawn raids in April 1969, most were imprisoned on unattainable $100,000 bonds. (Some defendants remained at large; some were incarcerated on other charges.)

Outside the courthouse, several hundred supporters chanted fist-pumping rallying cries of "Power to the people!" Inside, New York State Supreme Court Justice John M. Murtagh presided as best he could. But within 30 minutes, defendants' defiant outbursts and spectators' unruly behavior disrupted the proceedings.

1970

Lumumba Abdul Shakur, Black Panther Party ringleader, was one of the New York Panther 21. Lumumba lived with defendant Afeni Shakur. ILLUSTRATION BY RICHARD TOMLINSON, *THE RICHARD TOMLINSON COURTROOM DRAWINGS COLLECTION*, JOHN JAY COLLEGE OF CRIMINAL JUSTICE

Panther ringleader Lumumba Abdul Shakur raised his fist, shouting, "Down with U.S. imperialism!" Supporters called for the removal of "press pigs" so defendants' family members could have their seats.

Judge Murtagh called recesses and periodically cleared the courtroom. On the second day, brawls erupted between prisoners and guards. Tomlinson saw court officers put down a troublemaker with their night sticks. "If a court officer got hurt, it got really nasty for the prisoner," Tomlinson said.

Richard Moore, a.k.a. Dhoruba Bin Wahad, jumped bail in February 1971, reportedly fleeing to Algeria with co-defendant Michael Tabor. Tried in absentia, Moore/Wahad returned to the U.S. after the Panther 21 acquittals. He was convicted on separate charges in 1973, and sentenced to 25 years to life for the attempted murder of two police officers. His conviction was overturned in 1990. ILLUSTRATION BY RICHARD TOMLINSON, *THE RICHARD TOMLINSON COURTROOM DRAWINGS COLLECTION*, JOHN JAY COLLEGE OF CRIMINAL JUSTICE

Although Tomlinson covered the Panther 21 conspiracy case for two years, there were times he questioned whether courtroom art was the right career move.

> "It was an unnerving first experience. If this was going to be a regular thing, I wasn't sure I wanted to be a part of it."
> —RICHARD TOMLINSON ON THE BRAWLS DURING THE NEW YORK PANTHER 21 PRE-TRIAL HEARINGS

"Artistically, the Panthers were a real challenge," he said. "No falling asleep in that courtroom. The defendants would suddenly jump up and yell, 'Power to the People!' Supporters yelled back, then it started. Court officers running in swinging clubs, knocking down any standing defendants, then dragging them to the lockup. All happening so fast, in a blur of movement."

A quiet moment for court officers at the disruption-ridden Black Panther 21 trial in New York City. ILLUSTRATION BY RICHARD TOMLINSON, *THE RICHARD TOMLINSON COURTROOM DRAWINGS COLLECTION*, JOHN JAY COLLEGE OF CRIMINAL JUSTICE

7/12/72 JUDGE JOHN MURTAGH 100 CENTRE ST. NYC

New York State Supreme Court Justice John M. Murtagh looked reflective when Richard Tomlinson drew him in his office at 100 Centre Street in 1972 after the Panther 21 trial dust had settled. ILLUSTRATION BY RICHARD TOMLINSON

"We are going to turn this raggedy pig pen inside out every day." —RICHARD MOORE, A.K.A. DHORUBA BIN WAHAD, TO NEW YORK STATE SUPREME COURT JUSTICE JOHN M. MURTAGH

During recesses, Tomlinson said, "The press room was our base. We all shared the news desk space with the news reporters, heard the latest gossip, shared the phone, the co-ed toilet. It was a family. We added watercolor to our drawings if there was time."

The pre-trial hearings were interrupted when the judge's home was firebombed, but resumed on April 7. Lumumba Shakur stayed in jail, but thanks to church groups' fundraising efforts, Afeni Shakur—the former Alice Fay Williams of North Carolina, who changed her name upon moving in with Shakur in 1968—was released on bail. During that time she conceived a son.

Afeni Shakur represented herself in court. The trial began on September 8. Gerald B. Lefcourt, an associate of famed civil rights lawyer William Kunstler, was the lead defense attorney. Kunstler, then embroiled in the Chicago 7 trial, visited the courtroom.

The case against the Panther 21 leaned heavily on the testimony of three undercover cops who infiltrated the Panthers chapter. They described attending classes in guerilla warfare and bomb-making. They conceded that they never saw any police officers shot or any bombs detonated but testified to overhearing plots to bomb urban landmarks.

The Panthers saw themselves as political prisoners; law enforcement saw them as gun-toting thugs.

9/23/70 AFENI SHAKUR BLACK PANTHER TRIAL NYC

Afeni Shakur represented herself at trial. Her bail was revoked after Richard Moore and Michael Tabor jumped bail in February 1971. Tomlinson drew her on September 23, 1970, in the early stages of the trial and her pregnancy. She was shocked when in May 1971 Judge Murtagh released her to await the verdict. Eight months pregnant, she sobbed with relief. ILLUSTRATION BY RICHARD TOMLINSON, *TOMLINSON COURTROOM DRAWINGS COLLECTION*, JOHN JAY COLLEGE

After an undercover detective testified to hearing Lumumba Shakur call for using Algerian revolutionary tactics against "the pigs," a screening for the jury of the political film "Battle of Algiers" made for a curious and memorable day. "You saw the French torture the Muslims using electric shock treatment to get information," Tomlinson recalled. "Algerian women had bombs under their white robes then left them in public places where the French were. So, it was an unusual courtroom scene to see the Panthers dressed in white Muslim robes watching the film."

But Tomlinson's strangest moment came in the hallway when a man pressed a wad of bills into his hand. "The guy who offered me the bribe was an undercover detective . . . I had just drawn him on the witness stand. He'd seen me drawing him and didn't want his cover blown on TV, so he was offering me money. Had I taken it, it would have become bribery."

The political film, "Battle of Algiers," was screened for the Panther 21 jury. Some Panthers considered it mandatory viewing, tantamount to a blueprint for inner city rebels. Richard Tomlinson found it interesting to see the women in court wearing white flowing robes like the women onscreen. ILLUSTRATION BY RICHARD TOMLINSON, *THE RICHARD TOMLINSON COURTROOM DRAWINGS COLLECTION*, JOHN JAY COLLEGE OF CRIMINAL JUSTICE

In January 1971, Tomlinson drew disturbing evidentiary photographs of Panther 21 defendant Joan Victoria Bird, 20, a former student nurse. Battered and bruised, with a black eye and a swollen lip, she claimed police brutality.

> "We recognize that we will never receive any justice in the courts. We see only the spirit of the people, which moves forth to free the people from the injustices of the oppressor. All Power to the People!" —FROM JOAN BIRD'S WRITTEN PUBLIC STATEMENT, OCTOBER 1969

Black Panther Joan Bird, a former student nurse, looked pensive when Richard Tomlinson drew her on October 22, 1970, during her trial in Manhattan Superior Court. ILLUSTRATION BY RICHARD TOMLINSON, *THE RICHARD TOMLINSON COURTROOM DRAWINGS COLLECTION*, JOHN JAY COLLEGE OF CRIMINAL JUSTICE

"Despite sensitivity about police brutality," Richard Tomlinson recalled, "the prosecutor never placed any restrictions on drawings. During a recess, as long as the DA was there keeping watch, we could draw anything once it was placed in evidence with a tag on it. Say, a pipe bomb, bomb debris, a Kel Transmitter SK7 model. Even defense evidence, such as a photograph showing Joan Bird with a black eye, all puffed up. My drawing was seen full screen on the 10 o'clock news."

In February, four months into the trial, Richard Moore and his co-defendant Michael Tabor skipped bail and reportedly fled to Algiers. Bail was revoked for Afeni Shakur and Joan Bird. And Moore and Tabor were tried in absentia. On May 3, Judge Murtagh released Afeni Shakur to await the verdict. By then eight months pregnant, she was stunned and emotional.

Richard Tomlinson illustrated the photographs depicting the injuries of Panther 21 member Joan Bird, who claimed she was beaten by police. The defense presented the images to the jury at the New York Panther 21 trial. ILLUSTRATION BY RICHARD TOMLINSON, *THE RICHARD TOMLINSON COURTROOM DRAWINGS COLLECTION*, JOHN JAY COLLEGE OF CRIMINAL JUSTICE

11/2/70 PIPE BOMB BLACK PANTHER TRIAL NYC

From caches of weapons and explosives seized by police from Black Panther 21 defendants: a pipe bomb bearing a police evidence tag. ILLUSTRATION BY RICHARD TOMLINSON, *THE RICHARD TOMLINSON COURTROOM DRAWINGS COLLECTION*, JOHN JAY COLLEGE OF CRIMINAL JUSTICE

On May 14, all defendants were acquitted on all charges. The jury foreman read "not guilty" 156 times. Joan Bird cried. So did Afeni Shakur. She also shrieked with excitement. Some spectators screamed with jubilation.

A bitterly disappointed Assistant District Attorney Joseph A. Phillips found it hard to believe that six months' complex evidence could be properly evaluated and a verdict reached in a couple of hours. But it was over. The defendants and their friends, family and supporters exchanged hugs and kisses in the courtroom lobby.

A month later, Afeni Shakur gave birth to her baby son who became rap star Tupac Shakur. He was murdered in Las Vegas in September 1996.

WHAT A DIFFERENCE A RIVER MAKES: NEW JERSEY'S BLACK PANTHER TRIAL

Richard Tomlinson captured a different vibe at the Jersey City 3 Panther trial across the river in the Hudson County courthouse on March 26, 1970. Charles Hicks, Isaiah Rowley and Victor Perez allegedly machine-gunned the Fifth Precinct station house from a car in 1968. Incredibly, one officer's hat was shot off his head and another's nightstick was shot from his hand, but there were no serious injuries.

Tomlinson recalled the defendants as well-groomed and whispering to their lawyers. Even the spectators were quiet and attentive. Civil rights attorney Raymond A. Brown had told his client Isaiah Rowley, former Jersey City Panther minister of defense, he would represent him only if he could be assured of court-appropriate behavior. Assistant County Prosecutor John J. Carlin argued for the state before Judge Edward F. Hamill. Hicks and Perez were defended by Seymour Goldstaub. The trial ended without a verdict due to a juror's illness. The defendants then entered guilty pleas to lesser charges. Rowley was sentenced to two to three years. Hicks and Perez were set free with time served.

OPPOSITE PAGE, TOP: Jersey City Panther leader Charles Hicks (foreground) with his defense attorney Raymond A. Brown at the Jersey City 3 trial in Hudson County Courthouse, March 26, 1970.

OPPOSITE PAGE, BOTTOM: Jersey City Panthers (left to right) Isaiah Rowley, Charles Hicks and Victor Perez on trial on March 26, 1970. BOTH ILLUSTRATIONS BY RICHARD TOMLINSON, *THE RICHARD TOMLINSON COURTROOM DRAWINGS COLLECTION*, JOHN JAY COLLEGE OF CRIMINAL JUSTICE

1970 3/26 JERSEY CITY BLACK PANTHER TRIAL

1970 JERSEY CITY BLACK PANTHER TRIAL 3/26

CHARLES MANSON:

Helter Skelter Murders Grip Hollywood

The 1970 Los Angeles murder trial of hippie cult leader Charles Manson and several of his female disciples, one of the most sensational in U.S. history, was Bill Robles' first court art assignment, and his longest. Howard Brodie also covered the trial.

For Minnesota-born prosecutor Vincent Bugliosi, taking down Charles Manson and the Manson Family killers in the Tate-LaBianca trial was the ultimate career-making case. "He was difficult to draw," said Robles, "because there was nothing unique about him facially. But he was a powerhouse in court. The defense lawyers' closing arguments were very passionate but boy, Bugliosi's was a marvel. When he got up there, you could have heard a pin drop. He went through all the victims' names then into his closing and he was brilliant." ILLUSTRATION BY HOWARD BRODIE © ESTATE OF HOWARD BRODIE

Charles Manson's cunning met Vincent Bugliosi's prosecutorial skill at Manson's trial for seven murders. On the first day, July 24, 1970, Manson appeared with a bloody 'X' etched in his forehead. His three female co-defendants copied him, then his followers keeping vigil outside the Hall of Justice followed suit. ILLUSTRATION BY HOWARD BRODIE © ESTATE OF HOWARD BRODIE

Along with former choir girl Susan "Sadie" Atkins, 21, two-time high school homecoming princess Leslie Van Houten, 19, one-time Camp Fire Girl Patricia "Katie" Krenwinkel, 21, and lost soul Linda Kasabian, 20, Manson was charged with the gruesome murders of seven people and an unborn child. (His top lieutenant, Charles "Tex" Watson, was tried and convicted separately.) Over two sweltering nights in August 1969, Manson Family members slaughtered the occupants of two upscale Los Angeles homes and left eerie messages written in their victims' blood.

In August 1970, medical examiner Dr. Thomas T. Noguchi explained to the jury his diagrams of the Tate residence victims' wounds. He showed a diagram of the 51 stab wounds and 7 head blows received by Abigail Folger's lover Voytek Frykowski. While Dr. Noguchi told the jury what brought on death for the victims, Robles recalled, "The girls were chattering away, totally oblivious. Then they would stand up and go 'Sieg Heil' or whatever because Manson did it and they'd follow. He must have told them what to do through signals because they always, always mimicked him." ILLUSTRATION BY BILL ROBLES

The carnage shocked even hardened investigators. Robles, especially, felt the pressure: "I was just a young guy and it took its toll because I ate, slept and drank the case. I developed a stomach problem, but it was all nerves." Yet Robles captured one of court art's most iconic images—Charles Manson lunging over the defense table to try to stab presiding Judge Charles H. Older with a pencil.

MANSON GIRL #1. Susan "Sadie" Atkins admitted that she showed Sharon Tate no mercy when she begged her to spare her and her baby. Atkins said: "Look bitch, I don't care about you. I don't care if you are having a baby. You are going to die and I don't feel a thing about it." Assistant District Attorney Steven Kay called her "the scariest of the Manson girls." She wed in prison, where she died in 2010. ILLUSTRATION BY BILL ROBLES

"You have to have real love in your heart to do this for people."

—SUSAN ATKINS EXPLAINING TO CELLMATE VIRGINIA GRAHAM WHY

SHE STABBED SHARON TATE

MANSON GIRL #2. Patricia "Katie" Krenwinkel chased down heiress Abigail Folger, then stabbed her to death. The following night she participated in the stabbing deaths of Rosemary and Leno LaBianca. In prison, she earned a bachelor's degree and taught illiterate prisoners to read. ILLUSTRATION BY BILL ROBLES

MANSON GIRL #3. Leslie Van Houten, described by a police psychologist as a "spoiled little princess," told a police sergeant that "you couldn't meet a nicer group of people" than the Family. She told another that Atkins, Krenwinkel and Kasabian were the women present at the Tate residence but conceded that Kasabian did not kill anyone. ILLUSTRATION BY BILL ROBLES

Charles Manson on the witness stand but outside the presence of the jury in November 1970. ILLUSTRATION BY BILL ROBLES

The unfathomable depravity began on August 9, 1969, at film director Roman Polanski's rented "love nest." Sharon Tate, 26, Polanski's starlet wife, then eight months pregnant, was slain with her unborn child. Also killed: celebrity hairdresser Jay Sebring, 35, coffee heiress Abigail Folger, 25, and Folger's lover Voytek Frykowski, 32. Steven Parent, 18, was shot and killed while visiting the property's caretaker. Sebring was stabbed seven times, Folger 28 times, Frykowski 51 times and Tate 16 times. Some victims were shot and bludgeoned.

Manson stayed home that night but the following night he traveled with the killing party. Bugliosi believed that Manson entered Rosemary and Leno La Bianca's home, bound the couple and left, waiting outside while his disciples slaughtered the couple.

Convinced that Manson orchestrated the murders, chief prosecutor Vincent Bugliosi's goal was clear: convict Manson of multiple homicides right along with his acolytes. Bugliosi knew that Manson had a strange hold over his followers. They did his bidding whether participating in an orgy or killing innocents. Bugliosi's challenge was convincing a jury that while Manson didn't kill anyone himself, he ordered the slayings and deserved the death penalty.

> "I may have implied on several occasions to several different people that I may have been Jesus Christ, but I haven't decided yet what I am or who I am." —CHARLES MANSON

Like Bugliosi, Manson was 35. The 5′2″ self-proclaimed messiah was a failed actor/musician, burglar, car thief, pimp and manipulator who had spent half his life in prison. Bugliosi, a doggedly determined master strategist, was the perfect adversary.

The Tate-LaBianca murders ended the hippie era's benign, loving image, along with the peace of mind of many of Hollywood's richest inhabitants. The defendants provided Robles and Brodie with endless color. Robles noticed that Manson's wildly unkempt appearance seemed a little tamer post-arrest and pre-trial. He'd cleaned up and had a haircut. But then Manson carved a sinister, bloody "X" on his forehead right before trial.

Susan Atkins, Patricia Krenwinkel and Leslie Van Houten carved "X"s into their foreheads, and so did other Family followers dutifully camping outside the courthouse. Amid threats by Manson, Bugliosi and Judge Older were assigned bodyguards. Brodie believed Manson was acutely aware of his effect on others; he liked to relieve the tedium with staring contests—akin to mini power plays—at courtroom regulars and reporters.

Robles refused to play: "Manson could look right through you but I just looked away. I wasn't going to get into that with him. What was the point?" Brodie, in contrast, stared right back until it was Manson who became uncomfortable and broke the eye lock.

"Charles Manson fixed his gaze on a juror who looked jittery,
on a seasoned reporter who turned away, and finally on me.
His eyes wavered. Not mine. It was my profession to stare."
—HOWARD BRODIE

B. Robles

*Manson with
new hair & beard style — mid trial
Manson trial lated 9½ months 1970*

Charles Manson giving the infamous "Manson stare" from the defense table; a look observed by Bill
Robles, Howard Brodie, assistant district attorney Bugliosi and all in Manson's sight line.
ILLUSTRATION BY BILL ROBLES

Brodie, working with reporter Bill Kurtis, once saw Manson's followers skipping childlike down the hallways singing—while carrying knives. Manson had given each a Buck knife and demonstrated how to slit "a pig's"—or police officer's—throat. "I saw other Family members stepping out of the elevators," Brodie recalled. "The sheaths of the guys' long hunting knives were flapping against their fringed leather jackets, the sheaths of the girls' knives were flapping against their legs. I alerted security. A guard told me that since their weapons weren't concealed, they were not violating the law."

Bugliosi knew a Family insider could help cement his case. Demure, serene-looking Linda Kasabian, the mother of a small girl, became his star witness. She faced the same murder charges because she was present during the Tate murders and was outside the LaBianca home. The critical difference: she defied Manson by refusing to participate, telling him, "I'm not you, Charlie, I can't kill anybody." "She was just a sweet little thing," Robles recalled. "She was very pretty, rather like

MANSON GIRL #4. Linda Kasabian spent less than six weeks with the Family before the slayings. Since she refused Manson's order to kill and didn't physically harm anyone, she became the key prosecution witness in return for immunity for her testimony. She gave Bugliosi a real window into the Family's world. Eight months pregnant when she testified, she told lawyer Paul Fitzgerald that she initially loved Manson and "felt he was the messiah come again." The slaughter changed her mind. She was kept in solitary confinement from December 1969 to August 1970 when all charges against her were dropped. ILLUSTRATION BY BILL ROBLES

Mia Farrow, and very nice. I spent some time talking to her in Bugliosi's office."

Kasabian, eight months pregnant and granted immunity, testified she didn't report the murders for fear Manson would kill her. But looking into Voytek Frykowski's eyes as he died, she ceased believing Manson was Jesus Christ.

She told the jury that Manson tried to enlist new men to the Family by commanding the females to have sex with them. Bugliosi's case for Manson's dominance over the group was building.

> "God, the power Manson had over them all was amazing. It was power over misfits, runaways, dropouts and druggies. Young people without moorings." —BILL ROBLES

In response to Kasabian's testimony, Manson made a slicing motion across his throat. But Kasabian didn't back down.

Being led past the rostrum, Susan Atkins grabbed some of prosecutor Vincent Bugliosi's papers and tore them before he could grab them back. Some news reports said he took a swing at her, something Judge Older called absolutely false. Bugliosi wrote in his book *Helter Skelter* that he involuntarily muttered "You little bitch" under his breath, nothing more.
ILLUSTRATION BY BILL ROBLES

The workings of Manson's mind both fascinated and confounded Robles and Brodie. Manson simultaneously denounced those who stepped on blades of grass or picked flowers, but claimed that killing innocent people meant no more to him than drinking a soda.

Brodie viewed him more as "a delicate little man" than evil incarnate. He felt Manson was capable at times of making insightful comments. Brodie said he could not function creatively if he viewed Manson—or anyone else—as nothing more than a brutal killer.

"Hatred is not part of my life," Brodie explained. "I really believe in human beings. Oh, he would scare you, believe me, but he also really knew how to talk to people. Manson could say things that were profound, and I knew what he meant when he spoke. He said very wise things that would make you think—he said, 'I'm only what lives inside each and every one of you.'"

Robles didn't find Manson particularly menacing, either. "Not compared to L.A. serial killer Richard Ramirez, the Night Stalker. To encounter Ramirez at night would have been frightening. Sometimes Manson looked menacing and demonic, especially when he shaved his head and carved the X on his forehead, then turned the X into a swastika. But I saw the other side of it. He had a warmth, an inner quality, and I could see why all those people followed him. They didn't follow him because he was menacing. Absolutely he had charisma."

> "We wouldn't put a crazy man on trial in my country."
> —SWEDISH REPORTER, WHISPERING TO HOWARD BRODIE

Brodie felt as if he and Manson did a wordless dance in court. "I was always within 10 feet of him and he sensed when I was sketching him and actually posed for me," the artist explained. "He would hold his position until I silently signaled him that my drawing was complete. He'd really know that I was there. And intuitively he would really acknowledge me. He'd turn around at times. He'd want to be sure that I always had a clear view that was right for me."

It's rare that a defendant speaks to an artist but Manson once surprised Brodie by creating his own impressionistic portrait of him and walking over to present it. He requested one of Brodie's portraits in return.

Brodie felt indifferent to the women's zombie-like behavior. But, naturally curious, he invited Sandra Good, a Family member standing vigil outside, to lunch: "I'd talked to her and Squeaky Fromme outside . . . and heard them call the trial the 'Second Crucifixion of Christ.' At lunch, Sandy and I sat in a secluded corner of a cafeteria. 'You seem to really care,' I said, 'but how can you relate violence to love?' And I heard her account of their supposed motivation, and her opinion that government and big business leaders were the violent ones, not they."

The trial grew more bizarre when President Richard Nixon, during Linda Kasabian's testimony, declared Manson guilty.

Manson snatched up a *Los Angeles Times* before a bailiff could stop him and held up the offending headline for jurors to see. Judge Older was furious. The defense lawyers demanded a mistrial. Request denied. To Manson, it was an opportunity to criticize the Vietnam War.

"Here's a man who is accused of murdering hundreds of thousands in Vietnam who is accusing me of being guilty of eight murders." —CHARLES MANSON, OF PRESIDENT NIXON

President Richard Nixon referred to Manson as guilty while the trial was ongoing. The *Los Angeles Times* front page headline on August 3, 1970, read "Manson Guilty, Nixon Declares." Defense counsels' efforts to parlay his blunder into a mistrial failed. ILLUSTRATION BY BILL ROBLES

On October 5, 1970, Robles captured the trial's standout image. Manson, tense that day, grew agitated when Judge Older refused to allow him to cross-examine a detective. The judge threatened to remove him from the courtroom, leading Manson to scream: "In the name of Christian justice, someone should cut your head off!"

On October 5, 1970, Manson grew agitated when denied the chance to cross-examine a detective. He leaped across the defense table to attack Judge Older with a pencil but a fast-moving bailiff tackled him in mid-air. When he was removed to a cell, the female defendants stood and chanted in Latin until they also were removed. Bill Robles truly captured the moment. "Judge Older was very dignified, formal and rigid, really," Robles recalled. "Nobody could move, no noise, no fooling around. When I once knocked my color markers to the floor making a great racket, I wanted the floor to swallow me up. Thankfully, Older didn't react. Manson, however, gave me the 'Shame on you!' gesture with his fingers." ILLUS-TRATION BY BILL ROBLES

With that, Manson leaped across the defense table and lunged at the judge, brandishing a pencil. A bailiff brought him down. Deputies rushed to restrain him. Manson was secured in a holding cell, leaving the artists to ponder how the pint-sized defendant had leaped 10 feet. For Robles, Manson's leap was the ultimate creative challenge and opportunity:

"It happened in a split second and I quite literally had to freeze the moment. I guess Charlie didn't like the way things were going. Suddenly he was flying across the defense table, but a bailiff jumped on him during the lunge, tackling him in mid-air. The adrenaline kicked in big time and

I dropped whatever I was doing and started roughing out what I saw. Manson had flip-flops on and I drew them going flying. I finished the drawing with what seemed like supernatural powers and off it went to its place in history.

"I was so excited because the story was so huge. My illustration was the top story on the nation's number one news program that night; the 'CBS Evening News with Walter Cronkite.' What a thrill on my first assignment as a courtroom artist!"

The state rested its case on November 16, 1970. Three days later, the defense rested, too—without presenting any evidence. To their attorneys' dismay, Manson and the women then demanded to be allowed to testify on their own behalf. Manson later withdrew his request. However, Robles will never forget the way Manson looked when he made a statement on the witness stand outside the presence of the jury, and the light hit him strangely:

"A ray of light came in the window and shone on Manson when he took the witness stand. It never happened with anyone else. It looked almost religious. It was really fascinating."
—BILL ROBLES

After 42 hours of deliberation, the jury returned guilty verdicts for all four defendants. Waiting to learn if they would be executed, the Manson women still seemed under some kind of spell. When Manson shaved his head, they mimicked him.

Brodie often chatted to the followers camped outside court. And on February 9, after being shaken awake by a 6.5 earthquake that killed 65 people, he spoke to some women sitting on the sidewalk embroidering. One said she'd thought they were rolling downhill until she remembered, "Charlie told us he'd cause an earthquake."

Atkins, Krenwinkel and Van Houten didn't waver in their conviction that Mason was a messiah when they took the witness stand in the penalty phase. Ignoring their own plight, they sought to absolve Manson of all guilt.

On March 29, the four were sentenced to death. Months later, Charles "Tex" Watson was, too. Hearing Manson's sentence read, Brodie felt "the same way I do whenever anybody is given the death penalty: I felt empathy for him." But while Bugliosi later described Manson as seeming near tears, Brodie saw "no fear in Manson's face when the verdicts came in. No tears were shed by Manson or the girls."

On February 18, 1972, California's death penalty was briefly declared unconstitutional and the group's death sentences were commuted to life in prison.

Manson girls with
shaven heads later part
of trial.

After the verdicts and while waiting to hear if he would be executed for his crimes, Manson shaved his head. Defendants Susan Atkins, Patricia Krenwinkel and Leslie Van Houten (left to right) then followed suit in a show of solidarity. Against their lawyers' advice, the women wanted to testify that they and not Manson planned and committed the murders.
ILLUSTRATION BY BILL ROBLES

Manson during latter stages of of his trial— note bald head.
Bill Robles

Charles Manson was found guilty of seven counts of murder and one count of conspiracy to commit murder and sentenced to death. California's 1972 suspension of the death penalty led to his death sentence being permanently overturned. Instead, he was sentenced to life in prison. ILLUSTRATION BY BILL ROBLES

WATERGATE: *Dirty Deeds in D.C.*

To artist Howard Brodie, being assigned to cover a story of Watergate's national importance "was an honor, I felt very lucky."

The first hint of dirty dealings in high places came with a bungled night-time break-in at Democratic National Committee headquarters in the Watergate hotel complex in Washington, D.C. On July 17, 1972, five men wearing expensive suits, ties—and surgical gloves—were arrested for copying documents and planting electronic eavesdropping equipment. One was a former CIA man, James W. McCord Jr., security chief of the Committee to Re-Elect the President, a.k.a. CREEP.

> "You get so many calls like that—burglary in progress—and 90 to 95 percent of them aren't anything." —POLICE SGT. PAUL LEEPER, ONE OF THREE OFFICERS ON SCENE WHO ARRESTED THE WATERGATE BURGLARS

The five CIA-connected burglars were indicted along with former FBI agent G. Gordon Liddy and former CIA agent E. Howard Hunt. Liddy and Hunt were members of the "White House Plumbers," Nixon's leak-plugging, covert investigations unit. During the burglary mission, they were assigned to CREEP.

President Nixon denied all knowledge of what his press secretary Ron Ziegler dismissed as "a third-rate burglary attempt." But mounting evidence—and tenacious reporting by *Washington Post* reporters Bob Woodward and Carl Bernstein—pointed to the Nixon administration's knowledge and approval. In one burglar's possession: a check from E. Howard Hunt.

The sprawling criminal campaign of dirty tricks that was uncovered involved wiretaps, money laundering, bribery, destroying documents, secret slush funds, character assassination and an "enemies list." Investigations and related congressional hearings led to a slow tsunami of criminal indictments, court hearings and trials. Nineteen top officials and presidential aides were sentenced to prison for Watergate-related crimes.

The most important Watergate-related trials Howard Brodie illustrated were those of the burglars and of the Watergate 7—key players in the cover-up that followed. The Watergate bur-

The Watergate "cover-up" trial that began on October 15, 1974, was a huge draw. The rather grand courtroom in federal court in Washington, D.C. was filled to capacity. ILLUSTRATION BY HOWARD BRODIE © ESTATE OF HOWARD BRODIE

glars' trial began in January 1973. E. Howard Hunt entered a guilty plea and served 33 months in prison. Four burglars entered guilty pleas five days later and did prison time. That left lead burglar McCord and G. Gordon Liddy, CREEP's financial counsel, standing trial in federal court in Washington, D.C. for conspiracy, burglary and wiretapping. Chief U.S. District Judge John J. Sirica presided.

Former FBI man G. Gordon Liddy (left) and former CIA man James McCord faced charges related to the bungled 1972 break-in and attempted bugging of Democratic National Committee Headquarters at the Watergate complex in Washington, D.C. ILLUSTRATION BY HOWARD BRODIE © ESTATE OF HOWARD BRODIE

To Brodie, the undercover officers known as the "bum squad," who patrolled the city in old clothes and a beat-up car, made colorful witnesses: "They were a 'mod squad' who trotted into court with red plaid pants, shaggy hair and muttonchop sideburns."

Liddy was calm and cheerful as he and McCord were found guilty on all counts. Then McCord wrote a bombshell letter to Judge Sirica hoping to escape jail time. He claimed that there was political pressure to plead guilty and keep silent, that there had been perjury during the trial and that others were involved. Sirica forced the investigation deeper. (McCord was sentenced to four months. Liddy got six to twenty years but only served 52 months.)

Public interest in the Watergate trials in federal court in Washington, D.C. was initially so high that hundreds waited, hoping to land a coveted seat. Artist Howard Brodie always enjoyed talking to die-hard trial-watchers. ILLUSTRATION BY HOWARD BRODIE © ESTATE OF HOWARD BRODIE

More dominoes toppled on April 30, 1973. H. R. Haldeman, Nixon's chief of staff, and John Ehrlichman, his domestic affairs advisor, resigned. And Nixon fired White House counsel John W. Dean III. Before a special Senate Watergate Committee, Dean reinforced McCord's allegations about administration involvement in the burglary cover-up and said the president was involved in hush money arrangements.

In televised congressional hearings, Dean said he warned Nixon at least 35 times that the cover-up was "a cancer growing on the presidency." Americans learned that CREEP destroyed documents linking Nixon to the break-in and that all the president's White House conversations and telephone calls had been secretly taped at his request since 1971. A long battle raged when Nixon refused to turn over those tapes. When the U.S. Supreme Court finally ruled that Nixon had to turn over the tapes, he resigned a few days later, on August 9, 1974.

Forty people, including three of Nixon's closest, most powerful advisors, were indicted by a federal grand jury in the Watergate "cover-up" case—*The United States v. John Mitchell* et al—for trying to obstruct the investigation.

Brodie recalled that the grand jury was kept busy for months. While speaking to them was forbidden, of course, "I sketched jurors on breaks outside their sacrosanct chamber."

"Women jurors are complaining about discrimination because
men are monopolizing the one restroom. That's the only leak."
—JUROR CONFIDING IN HOWARD BRODIE

The Watergate "cover-up" trial defendants included former Attorney General John N. Mitchell, H. R. Haldeman and John Ehrlichman. The House Judiciary Committee described President Nixon as "the unindicted co-conspirator."

Other defendants included CREEP counsels Robert Mardian (aide to John Mitchell) and Kenneth Parkinson. Chuck Colson, former White House counsel, and Gordon C. Strachan, a former Mitchell aide, entered guilty pleas.

Defense table overload: the defendants and a bevy of attorneys settled into federal court for 1974's Watergate "cover-up" trial. The key power players on trial were President Nixon's former Chief of Staff H.R. Haldeman (bottom left), former Domestic Policy Advisor John D. Ehrlichman (top left) and former Attorney General and Nixon campaign director John N. Mitchell (top row, extreme right). All were convicted and served around eighteen months. ILLUSTRATION BY HOWARD BRODIE © ESTATE OF HOWARD BRODIE

The Watergate 7's "cover-up" trial began on October 15, 1974, in a spacious, decorous sixth-floor courtroom in the Federal Courthouse a mile from the White House. During jury selection, most defendants looked grim. Ehrlichman sketched the courtroom's huge statues and bench conferences—and Howard Brodie, as Brodie drew him. Mitchell, with his distinctive jowls, sat off to one side.

Outside court, Brodie spoke to the trial groupies lining up for seats, including one who memorably wore a pink feather boa and a football helmet. Haldeman, Ehrlichman and Mitchell also sometimes stopped by the line to sign autographs.

Judge Sirica ran a tight ship and occasionally went on chewing gum patrol. Second gum offenses brought threats of expulsion from the courtroom. There were celebrity trial visitors, of course, including British actor James Mason and singer Johnny Cash. Brodie recalled being fascinated by a magazine in Judge Sirica's ante-room—"an advertisement for a judge's robe with a concealed fly front."

Chief U.S. District Judge John J. Sirica surveyed the courtroom from the bench. Seated below him were his court reporter (at left) and his aides (at right). ILLUSTRATION BY HOWARD BRODIE © ESTATE OF HOWARD BRODIE

Brodie sat on a foam rubber pad to help cushion the unforgiving wooden benches. The proceedings could be tedious; he drew jurors, a defense attorney and a couple of reporters battling heavy eyelids.

On several occasions, he began drawing Judge Sirica, believing the jurist's eyes just might be closing. But just as he was sure that Sirica's chin was sinking to rest on his robe, he'd have to stop. "Suddenly the judge's head would jerk back up and I didn't know if he had been deliberating or drowsing."

President Richard Nixon's former domestic affairs advisor John Ehrlichman took the witness stand at the Watergate "cover-up" trial under the watchful eye of Chief District Court Judge John Sirica. Testifying brought Ehrlichman to tears, Howard Brodie recalled. ILLUSTRATION BY HOWARD BRODIE © ESTATE OF HOWARD BRODIE

"Judge Sirica officiated with great equanimity, untainted by his celebrity." —AGGIE KENNY

When it was Ehrlichman's time to testify, his wife looked on. Noting the way her husband arched his brows and jutted his jaw, she sighed: "Now I see why news photos of John look so dreadful, but he only looks like that when he's concentrating." "Both brows pointed upward towards center," Brodie said, as Ehrlichman recalled asking the president to explain to his five children why their father resigned. "Tears filled his eyes. He wiped them away with his tie."

During breaks, the defendants took refuge in a nearby office suite. Incredibly, the court artists were allowed to join them—the only non-attorneys given such access.

"They didn't know how to cope with us," Brodie said with amusement. "They said we could stay as long as we wanted and we did."

As 1974 drew to a close and the jury deliberated, Brodie periodically checked in with the defendants. On New Year's Day, 1975, the third day of deliberations, "Ehrlichman and his wife sat on a sofa playing a parlor game. I sketched Haldeman, feet up on the sofa, knees tucked up, writing in a binder. Parkinson slept on a lounge chair. And Mardian and Mitchell watched a football game on TV below a big, hand-painted sign that read, 'Happy New Year'."

Suddenly, there were verdicts. Kenneth Parkinson was acquitted. Robert Mardian was convicted of aiding in the cover-up and his conviction was later overturned. Mitchell, Haldeman and Ehrlichman were found guilty of conspiracy and obstruction of justice-related charges. Ultimately, each served approximately 18 months.

Presidential counsel John Dean, who entered a guilty plea to obstruction of justice in October 1973, was sentenced to one to four years. His sentence was later adjusted for time served and he was imprisoned for four more months.

Aggie Kenny won an Emmy for her illustrations of the trial of former U.S. Attorney General John N. Mitchell and former secretary of commerce and finance chairman for the campaign to re-elect President Nixon, Maurice H. Stans. She drew John Mitchell when he took the witness stand. ILLUSTRATION BY AGGIE KENNY

THE MITCHELL-STANS TRIAL

In February 1974, while former U.S. Attorney General John N. Mitchell awaited the Watergate 7's cover-up trial, he was tried on separate charges with Maurice H. Stans, Richard Nixon's former secretary of commerce. The two former cabinet ministers were accused of acting to block a Securities and Exchange Commission investigation of fugitive financier Robert L. Vesco in return for a large campaign contribution from Vesco.

Aggie Kenny was on assignment for CBS in the Manhattan Federal Courthouse in New York. U.S. District Court Judge Lee Gagliardi presided.

"Maurice Stans was quiet," said Kenny. "And somehow he managed to disappear into the background, even in this high-profile trial. John Mitchell was easier to capture with his large frame, small eyes, prominent nose and droll demeanor."

The two men's attorneys were formidable opponents for chief prosecutor John R. Wing and his team of young government lawyers. Mitchell's patrician, silver-haired attorney Peter Fleming Jr. was relaxed, calm, and given to lounging at the defense table with a foot planted on a wastebasket. Stans' counsel Walter J. Bonner was more combative, a terrier-like table thumper.

Although Kenny's art won her an Emmy, it was a stressful trial for the artists present. They had no assigned seats, no front row vantage points and no choice but to jockey with reporters for position. "We were sometimes so far away from the action," she said, "that the witnesses were almost totally obstructed from view. The best vantage points offered half the witnesses' faces—the top half! We could only see them from the nose up.

"A lot of us ended up using opera glasses. It was a real battle of nerves," Kenny said.

Defense attorneys threw doubt on the credibility of witnesses like John Dean, and Mitchell and Stans were found not guilty.

"I felt honored to be recognized by the Academy," Kenny said of her Emmy. "I was young and I was intimidated by all the CBS executives, reporters, producers and directors seated at my table at the awards ceremony. But I do remember seeing Bill Moyers and Big Bird at the adjoining table—an interesting juxtaposition! The ceremony was televised and seeing my name suddenly appear in lights on stage was an exciting moment for me and my family."

PATTY HEARST: *Heiress as Urban Guerilla*

"The quiet was eerie," Howard Brodie said of the day in 1976 when kidnapped heiress Patricia Hearst testified at her San Francisco trial for armed bank robbery. "Jurors, press, spectators strained to hear her softly tell of terrorists imprisoning her in a hot closet inside a house. She spoke of Cinque, the leader, saying she was a prisoner of war and telling her that if she made any noise they'd hang her up from the ceiling."

Bill Robles remembered publishing magnate William Randolph Hearst's granddaughter as "very delicate, very petite and a paradox, really. But I felt a lot of compassion for her."

Patty Hearst, 19, a college student making wedding plans, casually opened her apartment door on February 4, 1974. Masked gunmen barged inside. She was bundled up and whisked away. She was held captive in various apartment closets for weeks, often denied access to a bathroom.

She was kidnapped by members of the obscure but violent fringe group, the Symbionese Liberation Army (SLA), blamed for the earlier murder of Oakland, California, Schools Superintendent Marcus Foster. The SLA's list of goals included overthrowing the U.S. government.

Randolph and Catherine Hearst received a tape recording of their terrified daughter begging her father to meet her captors' demands. One request: that he provide millions of dollars' worth of food for the poor.

But Hearst's innocent hostage/political prisoner persona took a nosedive a few weeks later. She took up arms alongside her kidnappers in the April 15 robbery of a branch of Hibernia Bank in San Francisco during which two bystanders were shot.

She was caught on tape brandishing a weapon. Police also received a photograph of her in urban guerilla gear, standing before the SLA's seven-headed cobra flag, wielding a sub-machine gun. Calling herself "Tania," she announced on tape that she'd joined the SLA and had voluntarily robbed the bank with her comrades to finance "the revolution."

Initially, most believed that if Patty Hearst hadn't been kidnapped, there would have been no bank robbery. But was she really under duress? Was her life really being threatened? It didn't help when she coldly dismissed her teacher fiancé Steven Weed as a "sexist pig" and her parents as "pigs" and "clowns." The public divided over her culpability.

Heiress Patty Hearst took the witness stand in federal court in San Francisco in February 1976 at her trial on armed rob-bery charges for her role in the Symbionese Liberation Army hold-up at a branch of Hibernia Bank. ILLUSTRATION: BILL ROBLES/NEWSWEEK

Patty Hearst's weapon was key evidence for U.S. Attorney James L. Browning during her trial in federal court in San Francisco for her role in the Hibernia Bank robbery. While Hearst was on the witness stand in February 1976, Browning, seen here addressing the jury, handed her a sawn-off, semi-automatic rifle. She identified it as her weapon. ILLUSTRATION: HOWARD BRODIE, CBS NEWS/*NEW YORK TIMES* © ESTATE OF HOWARD BRODIE

In May, Patty Hearst was in Inglewood, Los Angeles, in a van across from Mel's Sporting Goods store waiting for SLA members Bill and Emily Harris. Bill Harris scuffled with a security guard while trying to shoplift a pair of socks, and Patty sprang into action. She opened fire at the store window with a semi-automatic weapon to cover the Harrises' escape. "Let them go, you mother-fuckers, or you're all dead!" she cried. Incredibly, no one was hurt.

> "She looked so fragile that it was hard to reconcile this
> Patty with the machine gun–wielding radical in the news."
> —BILL ROBLES

Later, Hearst said that escaping didn't seem a viable option. She was sure that either the FBI or SLA would kill her.

The day after the sporting goods store shooting, six SLA members (one a lover of Hearst's) died in a huge shootout with authorities at a Los Angeles safe house that went up in flames. The heiress was not among the casualties.

Howard Brodie described the federal courtroom in San Francisco where Patty Hearst stood trial as huge, crowded—and eerily quiet when the heiress testified. "She practically disappeared in that vast courtroom," Bill Robles recalled. ILLUS-TRATION: HOWARD BRODIE/CBS NEWS © ESTATE OF HOWARD BRODIE

She lived underground for some 19 months before being arrested in San Francisco with the Harrises on September 18, 1975. In February 1976, she stood trial there for the bank robbery. U.S. District Judge Oliver J. Carter presided as spectators camped outside overnight for seats.

The Hearsts hired famed defense lawyer F. Lee Bailey to represent their daughter. Brodie noted the sharp contrast between the affluent Bailey's custom-made suits and U.S. Attorney James L. Browning's traditional tweeds, improbably paired with patent leather shoes.

"You still wearing your fag shoes?" Bailey snickered. Browning fired back: "You, your pimp suits?"

Browning was effective, Robles thought, "But it would be difficult to compete with F. Lee Bailey's charisma at the pinnacle of his career."

> "F. Lee Bailey was, of course, a dynamic, confident and skilled
> individual, and back then it was a pleasure to see him in action."
> —BILL ROBLES

Patty Hearst's defense attorney F. Lee Bailey (left) stood before Judge Oliver J. Carter with his client. At right, U.S. Attorney James L. Browning speaking for the State. ILLUSTRATION: HOWARD BRODIE/CBS NEWS © ESTATE OF HOWARD BRODIE

Brodie recalled watching "thin, pale Patty in a chic pants suit" being escorted to the defense table by marshals. Her parents sat nearby.

The Hearst trial was a somber affair in a grand courtroom, but the men's room was a great equalizer. Brodie chuckled on seeing Bailey tuck in a pink shirttail over shiny red boxers—a detail the artist sadly could not use.

Bailey told the jury that Hearst believed the terrorists would kill her if she didn't participate in the robbery. He described his client as "a particularly vulnerable, frightened 19-year-old" who felt "she had been abandoned by her society."

Defense witnesses spoke of mind control, brainwashing and mental deterioration. Prosecution witness Dr. Joel Fort viewed Hearst as a willing participant, "a rebel looking for a cause."

Anticipation ran high when the defendant took the witness stand. But, Brodie recalled, even when describing her ordeal of being transported in a car trunk she was expressionless. When she spoke of being confined in closets, said Robles, "She was emotional but in a matter-of-fact kind of way. It was all so fascinating."

> "I was blindfolded and gagged, struck in the face. I lost
> consciousness." —PATTY HEARST

Hearst did shed tears describing sexual assaults. "Tears dripping from Patty's eyes glistened on her cheeks," said Brodie. Patty disavowed her statements supporting the SLA as coerced lies.

Some viewed Patty's parents as chilly, but Robles sensed their sympathy and concern for their daughter. "Although I didn't see any gestures between them, there just seemed to be a warm feeling between Patty and her family," he said.

Robles felt huge pressure to accurately portray Patty Hearst. "Her features are delicate and fine," he said, "which makes them rather difficult to capture. But she has a nice profile and her beautiful hair helped me get a good likeness. Randolph Hearst was very tall and handsome. Catherine also was very attractive. I found them quite easy to draw, especially Patty's father."

Years later, in a memoir, Patty revealed her dismay when F. Lee Bailey rambled in his critical closing argument and—given his flushed face and shaking hands—her suspicion that he'd been drinking. Bailey also knocked a glass of water off the podium. It hit him in the crotch, Brodie recalled, leaving him looking as if he'd wet his pants.

When the case went to the jury, the strain was too much for Catherine Hearst, who left the courtroom and sobbed, "I've chickened out."

> "Patty's parents looked as if they had been hit with bricks. I
> felt emotional for all of them." —HOWARD BRODIE

Marshals taped paper over the courtroom doors' windows in preparation for the verdict. Tension mounted. On March 19, 1976, the wait was over: "Guilty."

Spectators gasped and Bailey put his arms around his client, Brodie recalled. Her sisters wept. Her mother moaned, "Oh my God," and her father, "Oh Christ." Even Hearst's female marshal cried as the press stampeded outside. She was sentenced to seven years in prison.

> "I tried to convey Patty's parents' pain and agony. It was like a
> Greek tragedy. Their heads were buried (in their hands) after
> the verdict and they were sobbing." —HOWARD BRODIE

On March 29, 1976, Hearst was arraigned in Los Angeles on charges related to the Inglewood sporting goods store incident. Robles was struck by how delicate she looked, sitting alongside the Harrises. Neither party testified against the other but they seemed to avoid looking at one another. The tension was palpable.

Supporters' efforts to free Hearst paid off in November 1976. Robles saw Randolph Hearst and his brother in court in Los Angeles writing a $500,000 bail check.

In April 1977, when Hearst was out on bail pending her appeal in San Francisco, she entered a plea of no contest to the sporting goods store charges. Some charges were dropped and she was spared a second trial. In May, she was given five years probation.

By the time of her final full release, she had served less than two years. In 1979, President Jimmy Carter commuted her sentence. President Bill Clinton granted her a full pardon in January 2001. Patty wed her former prison guard, Bernard Shaw, and went on to live a quiet family life in the Hudson Valley with Shaw and their children.

Bill Robles vividly remembered *San Francisco Examiner* owner Randolph Hearst, accompanied by his twin brother, taking out his checkbook in court in Los Angeles. It was November 18, 1976. "It's not every day you see someone write a check for $500,000.00," Robles recalled. "That was a lot of money, especially in those days." The following day, Patty was released pending her appeal in San Francisco. ILLUSTRATION: BILL ROBLES, KCBS/KNXT TV

After pleading no contest in April 1977 to charges related to spraying Mel's Sporting Goods Store in Inglewood, Los Angeles with gunfire, Patty Hearst received five years probation. ILLUSTRATION: BILL ROBLES/CBS NEWS

DAVID BERKOWITZ: *The Son of Sam Murders*

On October 20, 1977, Aggie Kenny and Richard Tomlinson—two artists with distinctly different styles—found themselves on a highly unusual assignment. They covered a competency hearing for accused serial killer David Berkowitz, the self-proclaimed "Son of Sam," then being housed under guard in the psychiatric ward at Kings County Hospital in Brooklyn, New York. Security was so tight, the hearing was held in the sixth floor recreation room, transformed into a makeshift courtroom.

No one was taking any chances with Berkowitz, a pudgy, cherub-faced, 24-year-old postal worker. As the artists walked through several doors to get to the courtroom, each slammed ominously behind them. "The press was locked in with him," Tomlinson observed. "But as close as I was, I never spoke to him. No reporter did. In a situation like that, you just keep your mouth shut and draw."

And that suited Tomlinson: "I prefer not to know people that I draw on a personal level. It can become a kind of intrusion somehow, a distraction, in the sense that they become too real. I want to keep it more abstract in my mind."

> "Drawing David Berkowitz in the hospital was the closest I've
> ever gotten to a defendant. We were behind bars on that one."
> —RICHARD TOMLINSON

The August 10, 1977 arrest of this lethal loner could not have come soon enough for New Yorkers. In his year-long reign of terror, he killed six people—five of them young women—and shot and wounded seven others. The seemingly random murders scattered in Queens, Brooklyn and the Bronx immobilized many fearful city residents.

The killer ambushed women and couples sitting in parked cars on quiet streets or in lovers' lanes. His first victims, on July 29, 1976, were teenage friends Donna Lauria and Jody Valenti, who were shot while chatting in a car outside Lauria's apartment building. Lauria died, Valenti survived.

The brazen slaying triggered the NYPD's largest-ever manhunt. It took four shootings before police realized, through ballistics and the perpetrator's .44-caliber Charter Arms Bulldog revolver, that these seemingly disparate attacks were the work of one killer. In January 1977, a ".44-Caliber Killer Task Force" was established. By March, officials had publicly announced they were seeking a serial killer.

(10/20/77) DAVID R. BERKOWITZ , COMPETENCY HEARING , KINGS COUNTY HOSP.

Take One: Richard Tomlinson's view of "Son of Sam" killer David Berkowitz at the hospital competency hearing on October 20, 1977. Berkowitz appeared in a makeshift courtroom set-up in a recreation room at Kings County Hospital psychiatric ward in Brooklyn, New York. ILLUSTRATION BY RICHARD TOMLINSON, *THE RICHARD TOMLINSON COURTROOM DRAWINGS COLLECTION*, JOHN JAY COLLEGE OF CRIMINAL JUSTICE

Take Two: Aggie Kenny's view of David Berkowitz, the Son of Sam (left), on October 20, 1977 at a competency hearing presided over by Judge John R. Starkey. The temporary courtroom was set up in the psychiatric ward at Kings County Hospital, Brooklyn, where Berkowitz was held. ILLUSTRATION BY AGGIE KENNY

In April, the killer seemed to be taunting law enforcement by leaving a note for a police chief at a murder scene signed "Son of Sam." In May, New York's colorful columnist Jimmy Breslin, who wrote about the case for the New York *Daily News*, received his own taunting "Son of Sam" letter.

On July 31, Berkowitz crept up behind a car and shot Stacy Moskowitz and Robert Violante, out on a first date. Moskowitz died. Violante lost one eye and was left partially blind in the other. But police finally caught the critical break: a witness saw Berkowitz leaving the area and noticed a parking ticket on his vehicle. With news of his arrest, the public went wild.

Richard Tomlinson got word from Bob O'Brien, a colleague at New York's Channel 5 News.

"Reporter Bob O'Brien telephoned me at 3 a.m. and said,
'They've got Son of Sam!' Who could go back to sleep after
that?" —RICHARD TOMLINSON

Berkowitz was arraigned on August 11 in Brooklyn Supreme Court for second degree murder, attempted murder and assault. Outside, several hundred angry spectators chanted, "Kill him! Kill him! Kill him!"

Berkowitz's sanity was an issue. While he promptly confessed to the murders, he also claimed to be possessed by "howling and crying demons demanding blood." He said his neighbor Sam Carr's black Labrador retriever ordered the killing spree.

JIMMY BRESLIN

Tomlinson drew renowned New York *Daily News* columnist Jimmy Breslin in 1978. Breslin, who was covering "Son of Sam" for his paper, became part of the story, receiving a letter from the killer in May 1977. ILLUSTRATION BY RICHARD TOMLINSON, *THE RICHARD TOMLINSON COURTROOM DRAWINGS COLLECTION*, JOHN JAY COLLEGE OF CRIMINAL JUSTICE

At Berkowitz's October 20 competency hearing, Tomlinson and Kenny saw a presentation from Berkowitz's lawyers Ira Jultak and Leon Stern. Court-ordered psychiatrists Dr. Daniel W. Schwartz and Dr. Richard L. Weidenbacher testified that Berkowitz understood the charges against him, understood the legal process and knew that his acts were crimes. However, the doctors concluded that Berkowitz's "paranoid psychosis" rendered him unfit to stand trial in the Moskowitz/Violante case.

Berkowitz did not testify but he did interrupt. When Dr. Schwartz mentioned the neighbor's dog, he objected, "It was not a dog." And he contradicted Dr. Schwartz's opinion that he was deluded.

During the October 20 competency hearing, David Berkowitz sat with his bearded attorney Ira Jultak. Psychiatrist Dr. Daniel Schwartz (far right) initially declared Berkowitz mentally incompetent to stand trial. Later, he revised his opinion.
ILLUSTRATION BY AGGIE KENNY

"There is only one problem, doctor. They're not delusions."
—DAVID BERKOWITZ, INTERRUPTING TESTIMONY FROM PSYCHIATRIST
DR. DANIEL SCHWARTZ

DAVID R. BERKOWITZ

Richard Tomlinson found a fascinating subject in the Son of Sam, a.k.a. David Berkowitz, and aimed to capture the serial killer's evolving moods, state of mind and appearance in his portraits. He drew this one on October 31, 1977. ILLUSTRATION BY RICHARD TOMLINSON, *THE RICHARD TOMLINSON COURTROOM DRAWINGS COLLECTION*, JOHN JAY COLLEGE OF CRIMINAL JUSTICE

Aggie Kenny was drawing Berkowitz listening to the testimony when he spoke out, so she quickly scribbled his words on her illustration.

"In as much as we artists are not cameras and are unable to capture events frame by frame," she explained, "I try to record moments that tell the story. If something happens unrelated to the subject on my pad, I'll pull out a fresh piece of paper and draw the new event. Sometimes, the

(446) DAVID R. BERKOWITZ

David Berkowitz arrived at his May 22, 1978, sentencing hearing at Brooklyn Supreme Court with a cluster of court officers. He repeatedly yelled "Stacy is a whore!" He was referring to his victim Stacy Moskowitz, Neysa Moskowitz's murdered daughter. His outbursts caused the hearing to be postponed. ILLUSTRATION BY RICHARD TOMLINSON, *THE RICHARD TOMLINSON COURTROOM DRAWINGS COLLECTION*, JOHN JAY COLLEGE OF CRIMINAL JUSTICE

new drawing becomes the focus of the story. Consequently, I end up with stacks of unfinished, unused pieces."

Brooklyn District Attorney Eugene Gold won the right to have another psychiatric evaluation. Psychiatrist Dr. David Abrahamsen interviewed Berkowitz for a month before declaring his demons "a conscious invention" and finding him competent. (In 1979, Berkowitz told FBI profiler Robert Ressler—who pegged Berkowitz as a serial killer driven by anger over his problems with women—that his demonic possession story was a hoax.)

Richard Tomlinson, who drew a number of portraits of Berkowitz, noticed that once his wild-looking hair was cut, his constant scratching stopped. However, the artist was most interested in capturing Berkowitz's behavioral and mental metamorphosis—his transition from "be-

David Berkowitz shot and killed Neysa Moskowitz's daughter Stacy Moskowitz. Richard Tomlinson drew Mrs. Moskowitz in court that summer. A victim's mother's presence is often deeply felt but was especially powerful on May 8 when Berkowitz entered guilty pleas to all six murder charges. ILLUSTRATION BY RICHARD TOMLINSON, *THE RICHARD TOMLINSON COURTROOM DRAWINGS COLLECTION*, JOHN JAY COLLEGE OF CRIMINAL JUSTICE

calmed state in the hospital" to "manic antics" in court. Tomlinson tried to capture the changes "from hyper-manic to an enforced, doped-up stupor."

> "Berkowitz scratched incessantly. It began to make me feel itchy just watching him." —RICHARD TOMLINSON

Elizabeth Williams was fascinated by Tomlinson's and Kenny's takes on the defendant—drawn at the same hearing and moment in time. "Notice it's the same striped shirt in two of these illustrations," she said. "Richard was more focused on Berkowitz's demeanor and energy and on observing that he looked 'wild.' Aggie was more focused on his features and in her eyes, Berkowitz looked cherubic yet crazy.

"And interestingly, their art techniques married their interpretations. Richard's approach was more aggressive, digging into the paper with a charcoal pencil and creating an almost violent line that matched his perception. Aggie's reflections are often more composition-focused and she went for the big, wide makeshift courtroom scene, working carefully using watercolor and line. I think seeing their two takes on Berkowitz gives the reader a more complete picture."

At Berkowitz's next competency hearing in spring 1978, Drs. Schwartz and Weidenbacher reversed their earlier opinions and said he was improving with treatment. They did not suggest that he was sane when he killed, only that he was now competent to participate in his defense. Judge Joseph R. Corso declared him mentally fit for trial.

However, a trial was not in the cards. On May 8, 1978, Berkowitz pleaded guilty to all six murders.

Berkowitz had been almost eerily calm during the hearings in the hospital, but on May 22, when he was ushered into Judge Corso's courtroom for sentencing, Berkowitz suddenly careened out of control. Although he was surrounded by court officers, he caught them completely off guard.

He kicked, bit and scratched them before they could subdue him and chain his handcuffs to his belt. After a 90-minute cool-down break he was returned to court. But he immediately caused more havoc by chanting "Stacy was a whore! Stacy was a whore!" in a childlike, sing-song taunt. Neysa Moskowitz, the murdered girl's distraught mother, was livid, crying out that he was an animal.

Tomlinson drew the melee as officers once again swarmed Berkowitz and dragged him out of the courtroom. "That's right. That's right, I'd kill her again. I'd kill them all again," Berkowitz shouted.

On June 12, 1978, looking subdued, Berkowitz again went before three judges—one from each New York borough where there had been attacks. His hands were manacled to a wide leather belt around his blue suit and he'd been warned he would be gagged and put in a straitjacket if he again interrupted the proceedings. Each judge sentenced him to 25 years to life.

However, it was Stacy Moskowitz's friend Daniel Carrique's turn to cause a ruckus. He shouted, "Berkowitz, you're going to burn," before being dragged out and arrested. Over the years, Berkowitz has repeatedly been denied parole.

David Berkowitz's first sentencing hearing got out of control, so at the rescheduled sentencing hearing on June 12, 1978, in Brooklyn Supreme Court, he was restrained with a harness. Judges Corso, Kapelman and Tsoucalas, who had earlier accepted his guilty pleas, each sentenced him to 25 years to life for the relevant murders. ILLUSTRATION BY RICHARD TOMLINSON

JOHN DELOREAN: *"Let's Go to the Videotape!"*

On paper, it was a prosecutor's dream case, a slam dunk: incriminating-looking undercover videotape footage of automobile executive John Z. DeLorean in the thick of a major drug deal. DeLorean, 59, was a rich celebrity with a cover-girl wife—Cristina Ferrare, 34. His namesake gull-winged stainless steel car was famously reincarnated as a time-traveling machine in the Michael J. Fox movie, "Back to the Future."

The video certainly seemed to support the government's contention that DeLorean conspired to possess and distribute 51 pounds of cocaine potentially worth $24 million. "It's better than gold," DeLorean said over a celebratory glass of champagne.

He was arraigned in Los Angeles Federal Court on October 19, 1982, on drug conspiracy charges. But the case was anything but straightforward. The bust at Los Angeles' Sheraton Plaza La Reina hotel was part of a joint FBI and DEA sting. To DeLorean and his lead defense counsel Howard Weitzman, it was "outrageous conduct," a government frame-up.

Arriving at DeLorean's arraignment, his wife, Cristina, turned heads. "I will never forget seeing her escorted through the large, packed courtroom to sit in the well at a little side table beside her husband," said Elizabeth Williams. "John looked a little rough, unshaven, like he may not have slept. No tie, open shirt. Cristina was wide-eyed, hair pulled back and clearly in shock. She put her hand around his shoulder and spoke to him. It was a comforting gesture and I sensed that she was being very supportive. But the look on her face was tragic. That summed up the whole situation for me, so I had to draw it."

DeLorean led the Pontiac car company before age 40 and had also headed General Motors' Chevrolet division, but none of that mattered. To Bill Robles, stories of having and losing it all on a grand scale are mesmerizing.

"Arraignments are fascinating when they involve someone famous," he said. "You read about somebody like DeLorean, such an important figure with a beautiful TV star wife and a car empire, then suddenly the cocaine thing happens and history puts you together right there in the courtroom."

"The way DeLorean and Cristina looked at each other was very emotional and romantic. We had to capture that." —BILL ROBLES

John DeLorean, with co-defendants during their arraignment.

HETRICK / DELOREAN / ARRINGTON

A spruced-up John DeLorean was back in court to enter a not guilty plea on November 8, 1982. He was seated along-side—but did not look at—his alleged associates in the sting's "drug deal," William Morgan Hetrick (left) and Hetrick's associate Stephen Lee Arrington (right). Unlike DeLorean, they had been behind bars since their arrest. Also unlike De-Lorean, they entered guilty pleas to the charges against them. Hetrick was sentenced to 10 years in prison, Arrington to 5 years. ILLUSTRATION: BILL ROBLES/KNXT/CBS NEWS

Famed automaker John Z. DeLorean was arraigned on October 19, 1982, in Los Angeles Federal Court. "All eyes were on his gorgeous model/TV personality wife Cristina Ferrare, who was wearing a dark blue pants suit," said Williams. "She was escorted to a seat behind her husband and immediately rushed to his side at the defense table to talk with him and comfort him." He was released on bail. ILLUSTRATION: ELIZABETH WILLIAMS/ KNBC NEWS

"I was very upset," Elizabeth Williams admitted, "because I was young and new to the business and I really felt compassion for them both. My emotions weren't as in check then. Now I am more hardened. But it was one of the most emotional arraignments I had covered. I wrote on my drawing: 'packed courtroom, the most incredible day in my life . . . so intense . . . feeling compassion.' We are supposed to turn off our feelings but because I was so young, this one really got me."

DeLorean's drug-related legal woes had begun several months earlier when he met James Hoffman, a convicted drug smuggler and (unbeknown to him) a government informant. DeLorean was desperate and ripe for the picking. The British government had invested more than $140 million in his Belfast sportscar factory, but in 1982 the company was declared insolvent. DeLorean needed money fast.

The government alleged DeLorean, through Hoffman, hoped to save his company by buying and reselling drugs.

FBI agent Benedict J. Tisa was critical to the convoluted set-up, posing as a crooked banker willing to fund the deal. (Bill Robles recalled DeLorean's attorney Howard Weitzman addressing Tisa as "Mr. Crooked Banker.") When DeLorean said he had no cash to invest, through Tisa the government acted to keep the deal alive. DeLorean never did put any cash into the deal he was charged with funding. And on the various videos and audiotapes, he didn't directly mention drugs either, but rather the cocaine code word "monkeys."

FBI Agent Benedict Tisa went undercover as a corrupt banker in the FBI-DEA sting operation that snared DeLorean. Bill Robles drew Assistant U.S. Attorneys James Walsh (far left) and Robert Perry (leaning back) observing Tisa's cross-examination by DeLorean's attorney Howard Weitzman. This illustration preceded Perry leaning so far back he flipped his chair over. ILLUSTRATION: BILL ROBLES/KNXT NEWS

Weitzman conceded that DeLorean was referring to cocaine with the word "monkeys" and that his client had shown bad judgment, but asserted the government sting had pushed him to do it. Weitzman, said Robles, exuded confidence and paraded around as if he owned the courtroom. He seemed confident that he could put the government in the hot seat, showing his client as an innocent ensnared in an ethically dubious trap.

DeLorean's trial began in Los Angeles' Federal Court on April 18, 1984, with Judge Robert J. Takasugi presiding. Bill Robles was immediately intrigued by the 6′4″ DeLorean's dashing blend of elegance, good looks and charisma.

"My first thought was how very imposing he was, how distinguished-looking," he said. Williams was equally captivated by the beauty and glamour of Ferrare, DeLorean's third wife. (Ferrare once approached Robles in the cafeteria and said he reminded her of her first husband.)

Two heavyweight narcotics prosecutors, James Walsh Jr. and Robert Perry, went up against DeLorean's counsel, Weitzman and Donald Re.

Pivotal to the case against Cristina Ferrare's husband was undercover videotape footage of his meeting with William Morgan Hetrick, an aircraft owner federal agents described as a drug smuggler. "Seeing Cristina watching her husband in that powerful videotape when the jury viewed it was an obviously newsworthy scene," said Williams. ILLUSTRATION: ELIZABETH WILLIAMS/KABC NEWS

Weitzman argued that DeLorean was unaware he'd gotten himself involved in a drug deal until it was too late; DeLorean claimed that he wanted out but Hoffman had threatened to harm him and his daughter. DeLorean was heard on tape telling Tisa that he no longer had the money to buy into the deal. In counterpoint, Hoffman was heard on tape telling DeLorean that he could back out if he was not comfortable. DeLorean elected to proceed.

On the witness stand, Benedict Tisa conceded that DeLorean had put up no money and that the government had engineered a way for DeLorean to be able to participate in the drug deal—Tisa, the "crooked banker," would fund it in return for DeLorean company stock.

Six artists were assigned seats. Williams recalled the 22-week trial engendering a spirit of cooperation. "We'd switch seats so everybody got a chance to sit in the different spots," she explained. "Drawing the same subjects over and over again, I really got to know the characters. It was like playing scales on a piano and it really helped me develop my style and technique."

Cristina Ferrare often sat alongside her friend Margaret Weitzman, wife of DeLorean's attorney Howard Weitzman, or Cristina's mother, Renata, another fashion-plate presence. She showed her designer friend Albert Capraro's beautiful clothes to the world, albeit in the courtroom rather than on the red carpet. ILLUSTRATION: ELIZABETH WILLIAMS/KABC NEWS

Williams' fascination with Cristina Ferrare didn't diminish over time. "I had always considered her one of the most gorgeous models ever and one of my favorites," she noted. "And even though she was not the main event, drawing her every day wearing so many lovely Albert Capraro outfits was a delight and I've never had such an opportunity since. It was also a big deal—a fashion story. It's the only time I've ever seen a defendant's wife model clothes every day like a fashion designer's muse." Ferrare accessorized her colorful outfits with matching purses, jewelry and sunglasses from her own design line.

Williams added: "I have always found attractive people like Martha Stewart, the DeLoreans, John Gotti and Donald Trump inspiring. Beauty is always fascinating to me. It's aesthetically compelling. And Cristina's mother, Renata, who often sat with her, also was a beauty."

"It was such a treat for me. Beautiful model, beautiful clothes." —ELIZABETH WILLIAMS

Williams and Robles knew DeLorean was nervous. "We both noticed his hands behind his back twitching away," Robles recalled. "During the trial, his facial muscles twitched like involuntary movements: his eyebrows went up and down, his chin twitched. It made it tough at times to get a good likeness." For Williams, DeLorean's twitching was overshadowed by Weitzman's fidgety co-counsel Donald Re; she finds people who never stop moving difficult to draw.

"He never stood at the lectern," she explained. "He paced back and forth in the well of the courtroom like a caged animal. Finally I told him that if he ever wanted a decent drawing done, he'd have to stand still for at least a minute. I implored him. He promised to try but started pacing again as soon as the court reconvened. He must have seen my exasperated expression because once as he paced towards me he actually chuckled. But he still kept on pacing."

Gesturing and gesticulating were Weitzman's trademarks. "Sometimes he worked himself into a frenzy when making a point," Williams recalled. "He was relentless. Tenacious. Like a pit bull."

By contrast, the prosecutors were very still, quiet and serious in demeanor. However, Assistant U.S. Attorney Robert Perry did have a dangerous habit of leaning far back in his chair.

"And one day, he tipped it back just that bit too far," said Williams, "and it finally fell right over, crashing to the ground and taking him with it. The whole court and audience broke out in laughter. He was completely embarrassed, of course. He sat upright after that."

As the case drew to a close, tensions rose. "Cristina didn't ever cry," said Williams. "But I hurried to draw her as she doubled over with nausea during closing arguments. They had to call a nurse and the proceedings were briefly halted."

DELOREAN TRIAL   FINAL ARGUMENTS   DEFENSE ATTY. WEITZMAN 8/84

DeLorean looked on as his attorney Howard Weitzman delivered a stirring closing argument on August 7, 1984. But Weitzman's trademark animated gestures created a challenge for the artists because they must "simultaneously capture movement and emotion," said Williams. ILLUSTRATION BY ELIZABETH WILLIAMS

"Capturing any kind of emotional meltdown or outburst is an absolute must." —ELIZABETH WILLIAMS

"Everybody thought DeLorean was going down," Williams continued. "We'd discussed it in the cafeteria and I was definitely in the minority in the press corps in thinking he would get off. But I thought there was reasonable doubt." For Bill Robles, guilt was assured with that "better than gold" remark on video: "When I saw that, I said, 'Goodbye!'"

On August 16, 1984, DeLorean was acquitted on all counts. The jury apparently decided that the sting crossed the line.

"So many thought it was a long-shot defense, although I felt that his lawyer made a good case," said Williams. "The clerk almost said 'guilty' before she said 'not guilty,' as if she, too, was really geared up for a guilty verdict! The prosecution and so many others were so sure they had him."

If drama is a courtroom staple, the reading of a verdict can be, said Williams, like the resolution of a great mystery. Emotional reactions run the gamut from gasps of shock to tears or, sometimes, an eerie calm.

"Here," she said, "there was an outburst of elation from the defense while the prosecution sat quietly. It was a real shocker. Once the jury is excused there is an unbelievable rush out of the courtroom. Courts are so staid and quiet that it's incredible to see this pandemonium at the end of a trial."

"Drawing a verdict reminds me of being pushed off a cliff
with a parachute. Can you pull the rip cord in time?"
—ELIZABETH WILLIAMS

The joyful embrace that said it all: John DeLorean's acquittal on August 16, 1984. But the couple's happiness was short-lived. Cristina filed for divorce two months later and their 12-year marriage ended in 1985. Williams "felt very odd" covering a divorce hearing with DeLorean and Ferrare seated in opposite corners of a courtroom, their marriage torn apart. Cristina later wed entertainment executive Tony Thomopoulos. DeLorean died in 2005 at age 80. ILLUSTRATION: BILL ROBLES/KNXT NEWS

THE MAFIA TRIALS: *Bringing Down the Bosses*

In the 1980s, New York's "big five" organized crime families were feeling fierce heat. A massive law enforcement effort was aimed at the Bonnanos, the Colombos, the Gambinos, the Genoveses and the Luccheses. Between 1981 and 1987, more than 1,000 mafia family members and associates were put behind bars. Electronic surveillance was a cornerstone of many victories.

Rudolph Giuliani, then U.S. attorney for the Southern District of New York, was on the frontlines of the war on organized crime, along with Assistant U.S. Attorneys Diane Giacalone and John Gleeson in the Eastern District of New York, which includes Brooklyn.

Covering a variety of mob cases, artists Richard Tomlinson, Aggie Kenny and Elizabeth Williams grew accustomed to spotting characters like Carmine "The Snake" Persico and Anthony "Fat Tony" Salerno around Manhattan's Federal Courthouse.

"Some looked as if they were straight out of Central Casting for Francis Ford Coppola's movie, 'The Godfather.' Their faces were brimming with so much character, they just about drew themselves," said Williams.

Drug trafficking historically had been taboo, if not a death sentence, for those in old-school crime families led by mobsters such as Paul "Big Paulie" Castellano, the reputed head of the powerful Gambino clan. But times were changing.

In 1983, Tomlinson covered the arraignment of Angelo Ruggiero, allegedly captain of the Gambino family. When Ruggiero went on trial in 1985 in Brooklyn, a fellow defendant was Gene Gotti, brother of Ruggiero's close pal John Gotti, then an ascending mob star but virtually unknown outside the organized crime world. Ruggerio's drug-related activities meant he was very much on the outs with Castellano.

Because Ruggerio's recorded conversations linked him to Castellano, anti-racketeering (or RICO) laws gave the government all the probable cause needed to enter and bug Castellano's estate. The bugging led to many federal indictments. But for the artists, two cases proved especially compelling. First, Castellano's 1985 trial in Manhattan Federal Court. Castellano, Joseph Testa, Anthony Senter and 18 others were indicted in 1984 for, among other things, operating a stolen car ring and conspiring to murder two car salesmen.

When John Gotti stood trial in March 1987 in Brooklyn Federal Court, he was not alone. At the defense table: Diagonal front row, from top left: John Gotti, Anthony Rampino (a.k.a. 'Tony Roach') and the attorney for defendant John Carneglia, Barry Slotnick. Diagonal back row, from top: Gotti's attorney Bruce Cutler, informant Wilfred Johnson and his lawyer Richard A. Rehbock. After sitting near Johnson in court, Gotti learned that his "friend" had turned government informant. Johnson, who refused to join the witness protection program, was murdered in 1988. ILLUSTRATION: AGGIE KENNY/ABC NEWS

Angelo Ruggiero (left) was arraigned in Brooklyn Federal Court under the watchful eye of his defense lawyer Jeffrey Hoffman on August 23, 1983. John Gotti's reputed next-in-command allegedly ignored Gambino crime boss Paul Castellano's strong aversion to drug trafficking. He ran a huge narcotics network after the death of its founder, his brother Salvatore. This put Ruggiero and John Gotti on the outs with Castellano. Ruggiero died at age 49 in 1989, with four cases pending against him. ILLUSTRATION: RICHARD TOMLINSON / WNEW CHANNEL 5 NEWS / *THE RICHARD TOMLINSON COURTROOM DRAWINGS COLLECTION*, JOHN JAY COLLEGE OF CRIMINAL JUSTICE

RICO statutes carried penalties of up to 20 years, and gave prosecutors the leeway to pursue not only individual violations, but to show juries the whole tangled mafia web; it was a critical advantage in making their cases.

For example, Castellano's indictment cited a "pattern of racketeering activity" dating back to 1973, with charges including extortion, drug trafficking, prostitution and 25 murders. (Six of the 18 defendants didn't make it to trial. They were murdered first.)

While Castellano faced the music in Manhattan, Diane Giacolone's prosecution of John Gotti, his brother Gene, Anthony "The Roach" Rampino and Wilfred Johnson was ramping up in Brooklyn. Gotti's charges included loan-sharking and murder.

And big family trouble was brewing. Ruggiero and John Gotti were certain that Castellano would have them killed in retaliation for Ruggiero's drug dealings. And Gotti supposedly wasn't too thrilled when Castellano passed him over for promotion and anointed his former chauffeur/bodyguard Thomas Bilotti as the new underboss.

Mob boss Paul Castellano (far right, in spectacles) on trial in Manhattan Federal Court in November 1985 with alleged Gambino family associates Joseph Testa (dark hair, light jacket) and Anthony Senter (in tan jacket). Between Testa and Senter is distinguished, white-haired defense attorney Herald Price Fahringer. As the he was the Gambino crime family boss, Paul Castellano's murder trial was the focus of much media attention. At least, it was until he was gunned down in December outside a Manhattan steak house. ILLUSTRATION: ELIZABETH WILLIAMS/NBC NEWS

"Castellano had a commanding presence. A tall, striking figure, he walked right into court in his top coat, with a cigar in his mouth." —ELIZABETH WILLIAMS

Castellano didn't live to hear his jury's verdict. He and Bilotti were assassinated in a hail of bullets on December 16 outside Manhattan's Sparks Steak House. Four shooters in long trench coats and Cossack-style black fur hats launched a blazing crossfire that sent panicked holiday shoppers scrambling.

Gotti rapidly took Castellano's spot as Gambino boss. The FBI was sure Gotti had ordered the hit.

"There was little interest in John Gotti until after Gambino boss Paul Castellano's murder." —ELIZABETH WILLIAMS.

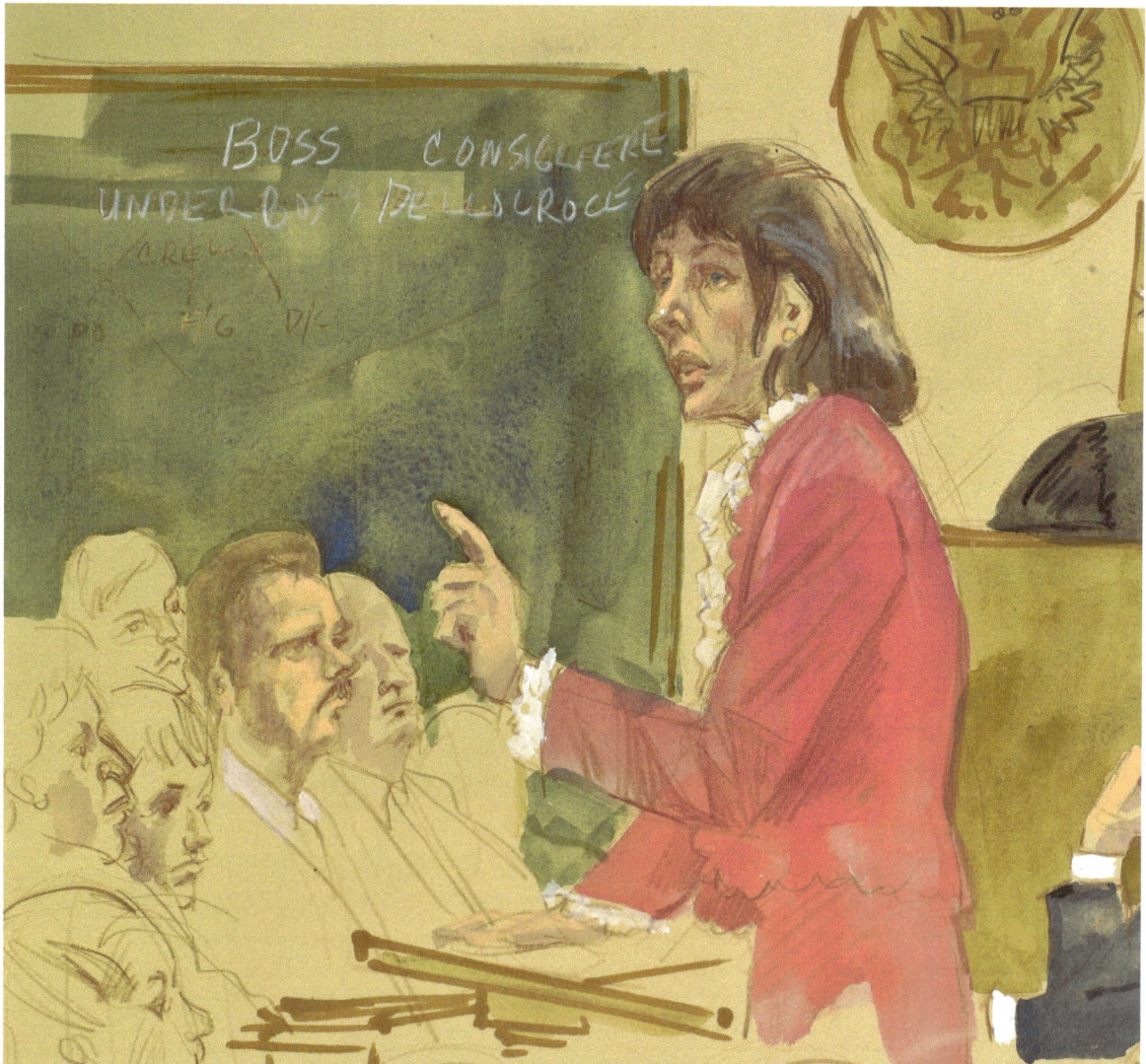

Assistant U.S. Attorney Diane F. Giacalone addressing the jury during the trial of John Gotti and his alleged associates in Brooklyn Federal Court in March 1987. Judge Eugene Nickerson presided. In this case, Gotti was acquitted, which caused jubilation at the defense table. ILLUSTRATION: AGGIE KENNY/ABC NEWS

With Castellano dead, NBC News dispatched Williams to the Manhattan courthouse to draw his empty chair.

"When I was done," she recalled, "I sat there finishing up an illustration of Castellano I'd begun the day before. Two men approached me and made it very clear they didn't like what they saw on my pad. 'Do ya have to draw that?' one said. I just snapped back, 'Look, I've gotta get my job done. I can't talk to you!' I was rushed!

"After they left, another artist leaned over and asked if I knew who they were. 'Lawyers, right?' I said. 'Uh-uh,' she said. 'Hit men.' I thought, 'Well, that is just great!' Rushing outside, I saw them again in the hall and one guy . . . well, if looks could kill! In retrospect, I realize they must have been pretty upset about Castellano.

"Mafia cases have a vibe all their own. And when I realized I'd spoken so sharply to two hit men, I admit, I was scared. That was my one and only really big oops. In their beautiful suits with every hair in place, they really did not look like mafia types. And this was back in the days when most mafia defendants weren't exactly smooth-looking, before John Gotti's sartorial splendor put a new image to organized crime."

> "The Castellano crew did not look like any mafia types I had ever seen before. Some looked more like a bunch of male models than mobsters." —ELIZABETH WILLIAMS

Williams' and Kenny's news editors dispatched them to Brooklyn to cover a hearing in the forthcoming case against John Gotti.

"Suddenly, there was a definite shift," Williams recalled. "Clearly our news editors knew that he was being anointed the new head of the Gambino crime family—even if I didn't."

Gotti's elevated position collided with the media's appetite for charismatic figures. He was stocky, handsome and dashing with a cool, imperious demeanor. Never mind that the Dapper Don's sartorial splendor—$2,000 tailored silk Brioni suits, $400 hand-painted ties—cloaked a ruthlessly vicious thug; the artists all loved drawing him.

Richard Tomlinson's take on illustrating organized crime figures did not involve nerves. "For me, the only mob presence was before me," he said. "Unless there was an outburst behind me, I tended not to be looking over my shoulder. The press helped to create this image of the mob."

> "I really never thought about these mob people as having star power. That's a Hollywood label, period." —RICHARD TOMLINSON

Williams viewed Gotti, whose ability to skirt guilty verdicts led to another nickname, the "Teflon Don," as intensely media savvy. "He was very conscious of his image. Few defendants interact with artists or really seem to care what we are doing. But I always sensed that mafia guys understood the process and saw it as part of the business." "There always was a polite little give-and-take on the elevator," Kenny recalled.

Williams remembered once working in solitude in an empty courtroom on a drawing of Gotti and his lawyer Bruce Cutler when she suddenly felt a presence behind her. "I didn't hear anything," she said, "so it was a strange feeling. Then I saw a finger point to my right hand. I looked up and it was Gotti. He said very sternly, 'Why aren't I smiling?' I said, 'Well, I have one at home of you smiling.' My mind was going about a hundred miles an hour."

Although she knew the truth about Gotti, she wasn't immune to his appeal: "I can think of no mafia figure to match his presence. Gotti had charisma."

Aggie Kenny felt a real incongruity "between this well-groomed, seemingly affable personality sitting before us and the death squad gangster being tried on RICO charges. It was so hard to believe that he had offed so many people, seeing him interact with others in the courtroom."

"Anytime you got a partner who don't agree with us, we kill him." —JOHN GOTTI TO FRANK LOCASCIO IN A WIRETAPPED CONVERSATION

Williams was in court in Brooklyn in late 1986 and early 1987 when John Gotti, his brother Gene, Anthony "Tony Roach" Rampino and Wilfred Johnson stood trial before Judge Eugene H. Nickerson.

Although family ties in organized crime were once all but indestructible, Wilfred Johnson turned informant on his old friend John Gotti. "Yet," said Williams, "sitting close to Gotti in court, Johnson was stone-faced. He just quietly kept himself to himself and showed no signs of nerves or anxiety."

In the previous six months, the heads of four other organized crime families had been convicted. This was an intense trial. Defense attorneys called government witnesses "liars" and "sewer rats." And when the defendants were acquitted, Gotti hugged his attorney Bruce Cutler while prosecutors Giacolone and Gleeson looked downcast.

Johnson, the turncoat, reportedly feared for his life yet declined to enter a witness protection program. He was murdered on the street in August 1988.

The mob trials weren't all murder and mayhem. Food chats were very popular at Gotti's trial when defendants congregated during breaks, often in the well of the courtroom. "They discussed with great relish and in great detail specific dishes and wines they'd had," said Kenny. "These guys were real gourmands."

John Gotti wasn't out of the woods. In July 1991, he lost Bruce Cutler, his highly prized defense attorney, pivotal in three of Gotti's previous acquittals. Cutler was removed by Judge I. Leo Glasser—"A very no-nonsense judge," said Williams—because he and two other lawyers were on secret recordings. Had those tapes been presented as evidence of Gambino family operations, the lawyers—whom Gotti once called "high-priced errand boys" on tape—might have been called to testify as witnesses.

John Gotti's defense lawyer Bruce Cutler delivered a powerful closing argument at Gotti's 1987 trial in Brooklyn Federal Court. "Cutler took the indictment—which was pretty thick—and threw it in a waste basket beside the podium," Williams recalled. "He was very theatrical." When John Gotti was acquitted at this trial "there was elation at the defense table," said Williams. Later, it was revealed that the jury was tampered with. ILLUSTRATION: ELIZABETH WILLIAMS/CBS NEWS

That October dealt Gotti a second major blow. His No. 2 and longtime friend Salvatore "Sammy the Bull" Gravano turned informant. Gravano was the highest-ranking mobster to flip. During nine days on the witness stand, he spilled details of the Sparks Steak House plot he and Gotti hatched to kill Castellano.

1991: finally, the so-called Teflon Don was going down. Elizabeth Williams captured this historic image of John Gotti and associates during their pre-trial hearing at Brooklyn Federal Court on July 26. It was the last time she saw Gotti with his attorney Bruce Cutler and with Salvatore "Sammy the Bull" Gravano. Cutler was removed from the case and by November, Gravano had agreed to testify against Gotti. Judge I. Leo Glasser presided. At the podium: Assistant U.S. Attorney John Gleeson. Seated behind him: U.S. attorney for Eastern District of New York, Andrew Maloney (taking notes) and attorney Herald Price Fahringer (legs crossed). Back row, left to right: bearded attorney Gerald Shargel, Thomas Gambino, Frank Locascio, Sammy the Bull, John Gotti and Gotti's lawyer Bruce Cutler. In 1993, Gotti was sentenced to life in prison. ILLUSTRATION: ELIZABETH WILLIAMS/WCBS NEWS

Williams vividly recalled drawing prosecutor John Gleeson (later a federal judge) at the podium in Brooklyn federal court on July 26, 1991. Four attorneys and their clients—Gotti, Gravano, Thomas Gambino and Frank "Frankie Locs" Locascio—were seated behind him.

"It was the last time I personally saw Gotti and Cutler together," she said, "and the last time I saw Gravano with them. They were never in court again, all together, seated at the table like that. By November, Sammy the Bull was testifying against Gotti and the other defendants. So my drawing could be one of the most historic pieces of art I possess."

Gotti was sunk when Sammy the Bull fingered him for the Castellano hit. Gravano testified for the government at eight more trials. He served less than five years for 19 murders he said he carried out for Gotti.

"Murder is the heart and soul of this enterprise." —ASSISTANT U.S. ATTORNEY JOHN GLEESON, PROSECUTOR AT JOHN GOTTI'S FINAL TRIAL

Gotti was sentenced in April 1992 to life without possibility of parole. He died in prison of throat cancer a decade later, age 62.

The artists relished their few lighter moments on the organized crime beat. Aggie Kenny cited the plight of presiding Judge Pierre LeVal at the 1985 Pizza Connection case, which busted a billion-dollar drug network using pizzerias as heroin distribution points.

"The poor judge," she said, "seated in this massive, ornate courtroom in New York Federal Court absolutely filled with defendants, attorneys, jury and media with recording devices, had laryngitis. He was reduced to holding up flash cards as if in primary school. I drew him waving the 'Overruled' card."

Richard Tomlinson chuckled whenever he thought of once drawing a clearly very nervous mafia defendant: "He couldn't keep his hands from pulling on the chewing gum in his mouth and he had strings of gum stuck to the sleeve of his really expensive silk suit. He had no clue." Tomlinson did not draw that.

A DIFFERENT KIND OF DON:
COLOMBO CRIME FAMILY HEAD, JOE COLOMBO

Joe Colombo once famously said: "Mafia—what's the mafia? There is no mafia." He presented himself as a legitimate business-man and in 1970 founded the Italian-American Civil Rights League to fight government discrimination against Italian-Americans stemming from mafia stereotypes. That caused a lot of chuckling and eye-rolling among prosecutors and reporters.

Crowds joined Colombo's picketing of New York's FBI head-quarters that April. The League's first rally in June drew 50,000 people, most of them proud, hard-working Italian-Americans. The group's respectability rose, too, as organized crime figure sup-porters were photographed with New York's mayor and governor. Then in December, federal agents examined a Colombo aide's briefcase and found lengthy lists showing donations from no-torious mobsters. Support for the Italian-American Civil Rights League evaporated, and Colombo was shot in broad daylight at another rally in 1971. He was permanently paralyzed. Who or-dered the hit remains a much-debated mystery.

JOE COLOMBO REPUTED MAFIA LEADER

Joe Colombo in court on December 18, 1970. ILLUSTRATION BY RICHARD TOMLINSON, *THE RICHARD TOMLINSON COURTROOM DRAWINGS COLLECTION*, JOHN JAY COLLEGE OF CRIMINAL JUSTICE

PREPPIE MURDERER ROBERT CHAMBERS:
Putting Victims on Trial

Robert E. Chambers Jr.'s 1988 trial for the murder of Jennifer Dawn Levin embodied two power-ful elements in criminal cases: the blame-the-victim defense and dueling expert witnesses. With its potent mix of sex, underage drinking, night clubs and privileged Manhattan teenagers, the so-called "Preppie Murder" riveted the nation. Levin, 18, was a college-bound brunette beauty, and Chambers, 19, was a dashingly handsome former altar boy. Behind the glib labels, however, lay the tragedy of a dead girl and a heartbroken family.

Williams and Tomlinson covered Chambers' hearings and his trial, which began in Manhat-tan's State Supreme Court on January 3, 1988. Aggie Kenny also spent some days in the court-room. The artists saw Chambers as cold and unemotional. Their challenge was simultaneously capturing his chiseled good looks and detached, empty quality. "He was quite expressionless throughout," Kenny recalled.

"Aggie's work really captured this 'missing chip' aspect to his personality," said Williams. "He looked very attractive and sleek but completely morally vacant. She nailed that perfectly."

Williams saw Chambers show emotion once: when his mother took the witness stand at a pre-trial hearing to determine if the jury would view his police interrogation tape. In it, he admitted to killing Levin. "His eyes reddened and he rested his head against his hands, watching his mother," she recalled. "That was it. Otherwise, he'd just shuffle into trial with his slightly hunched posture, then stay slumped in his chair all day, blank-faced. He was very wooden and stiff."

Jennifer Levin was murdered shortly after 4:30 a.m. on August 26, 1986. Chambers admitted they went into Central Park together after leaving a trendy Upper East Side bar, Dorrian's Red Hand. Having enjoyed a few casual "dates" with Chambers, Levin was, said a friend, smitten. Hours later, a cyclist found her partially-nude body amidst the trees behind the Metropolitan Museum of Art.

Chambers' attorney, Jack T. Litman, a former Manhattan assistant district attorney with a reputation for smear-the-victim tactics, faced off against Linda Fairstein, a tough prosecutor once called "hell on wheels" by the New York *Daily News*.

On February 9, 1988, defendant Robert Chambers watched the videotape of his police interrogation along with the jury. In it he claimed he killed Jennifer Levin by accident. ILLUSTRATION: AGGIE KENNY/ABC NEWS

Prosecutor Linda Fairstein found herself participating in numerous sidebars with Justice Howard E. Bell and Chambers' defense attorney Jack Litman—sidebars instigated by Litman. ILLUSTRATION: ELIZABETH WILLIAMS/WCBS NEWS

"They made for an interesting match," Williams recalled. "They both were very committed and passionate about their cases and causes. Litman was dogged when cross-examining witnesses. And he interrupted Fairstein constantly, really interfering with the flow of her case."

"Linda Fairstein was a determined and dogged prosecutor. A real fighter. And deadly serious when she entered that court-room." —ELIZABETH WILLIAMS

Fairstein scored artistic points with Williams "for her gorgeous blonde hair and for wearing dresses in nice colors that enlivened the dingy dark courtroom at 100 Centre Street. I was so grateful Fairstein wasn't, like so many female prosecutors, wedded to plain dark suits. So many female attorneys dress so drably, I want to cry. I remember Fairstein having a sunny yellow suit that really popped. She always was fun to draw with her fearless approach to color."

An uncomfortable juxtaposition: Jennifer's grief-stricken mother Ellen Levin sat right across the aisle from Robert Chambers Sr., the father of her daughter's killer. "This was a powerful image," said Williamson, "and Tomlinson immediately captured it." Mrs. Levin excused herself during the testimony of the medical examiner who conducted Jennifer's autopsy. ILLUSTRATION: RICHARD TOMLINSON/FOX 5 NEWS/*THE RICHARD TOMLINSON COURTROOM DRAWINGS COLLECTION*, JOHN JAY COLLEGE OF CRIMINAL JUSTICE

Williams found State Supreme Court Justice Howard E. Bell "fun to illustrate because of his great expressions and gestures. He got emotional and you could see him really pondering the issues during the sidebars and thinking things over. His expressive face was easy to capture compared to Chambers."

The case's "Preppie Murder" label was really a misnomer. "Preppie" is synonymous with "clean-cut kid" and Chambers was a college dropout, a drug user since age 14, and an alleged burglar. He entered a plea of not guilty to second degree murder. His well-connected family made sure he was out on bail throughout his two-month trial.

The jury viewed Chambers' police interview tape in court with Chambers and the artists. In it, the 6´4˝, 200-pound defendant claimed that Levin, a slender 5´7˝, instigated rough sex, bound his hands behind his back with her panties, then straddled and assaulted him. He claimed she painfully squeezed his testicles so he grabbed her neck from behind and yanked his forearm once against her throat to stop her. He insisted her death was an accident.

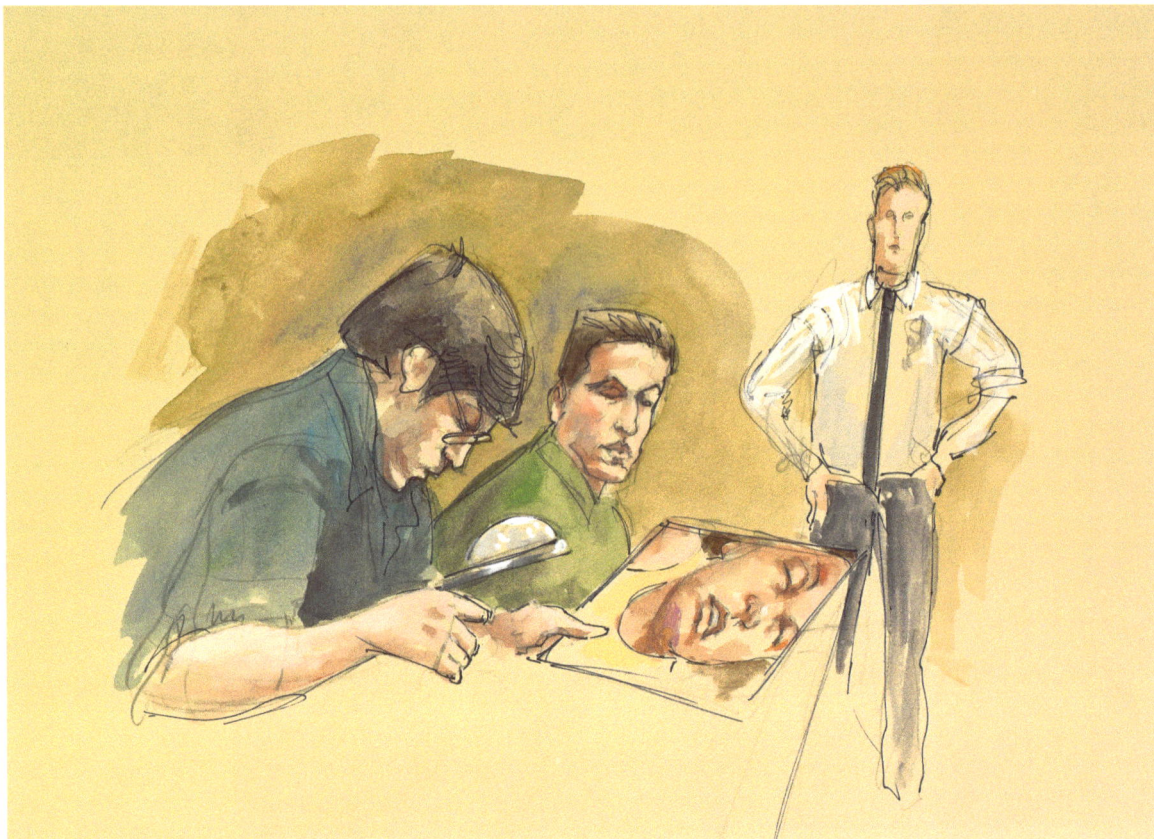

Jurors pored over a photograph of the marks on Jennifer Levin's neck. Their job: sort through experts' conflicting theories on how they got there. ILLUSTRATION: AGGIE KENNY/WABC, ABC NEWS

Chambers' rough sex story struck Fairstein as "preposterous." To her, the scratches covering Chambers' face, chest and belly—which he initially blamed on a cat and a sanding machine accident—bore witness to Levin's desperate fight for her life.

Litman doggedly tried to smear Levin's reputation. Noting that her clothing was not torn, he characterized her death as a "tragic accident" partly caused by her kinky sexual aggression.

Williams recalled the victim's mother, Ellen Levin, as a haunting daily presence: "She was very dignified and kept to herself, hidden behind dark glasses."

Fairstein called on Dr. Werner Spitz, Detroit's chief medical examiner, to help make her case for murder. He testified that Levin died by being strangled with her blouse twisted into a kind of "noose." Asphyxiation would have taken at least 30 seconds of continuous pressure on her neck, perhaps longer. In other words: no accident.

"There was only violence, only death." —PROSECUTOR LINDA
FAIRSTEIN, IN HER OPENING STATEMENT AT ROBERT CHAMBERS' TRIAL

But no expert could definitively explain the origin of two severe abrasions on Levin's neck. Kenny drew jurors studying photographs of the injuries with great concentration.

"I've drawn jurors poring over evidence ranging from a burned baby seat in an arson murder case to a black leather death mask and other unmentionable items used in sadomasochistic practices," Kenny recalled. "But it was very unusual to be seated so close to jurors inspecting such a graphic photograph of a murder victim. This image transcended any spoken word."

Dr. Spitz conducted re-enactments of how he believed the strangulation played out. To show "This was no sudden death," he held two models' heads from behind while twisting around blouses similar to Levin's and forcing them upwards to put pressure on their throats.

Without a good frontal view of the action, the artists struggled to see and depict this clearly. "He repeated the demonstration several times, but still it was tricky," Williams recalled. "Richard even took the rare step of drawing an arrow on his illustration to help clarify it for the readers and viewers."

A pink replica of Jennifer Levin's white blouse was draped across the lectern as prosecutor Linda Fairstein questioned Dr. Werner Spitz, Detroit's chief medical examiner, on February 24, 1988. He disputed Chambers' claim that he accidentally asphyxiated Jennifer and determined that her blouse was used to strangle her. ILLUSTRATION: ELIZABETH WILLIAMS/WCBS NEWS

Forensic pathologist Werner Spitz twisted a pink blouse similar to Levin's around a volunteer's neck, showing the jury how he believed Chambers killed her. ILLUSTRATION: RICHARD TOMLINSON/CHANNEL 5 NEWS/*THE RICHARD TOMLINSON COURTROOM DRAWINGS COLLECTION*, JOHN JAY COLLEGE OF CRIMINAL JUSTICE

Litman set about undermining Spitz's theory and in what the *New York Times* described as a "venomous exchange," dismissed the noose scenario as impossible. However, Fairstein made sure the jury saw the marks left on a model's neck by his demonstration.

Litman's defense witness Dr. Ronald Kornblum, Los Angeles' chief medical examiner, said Chambers' account of how Levin died was "consistent" with her injuries. He testified that her windpipe was not crushed and that she didn't die from frontal strangulation but from a chokehold from behind, just as Chambers described. Dr. Maria Luz Alandy, who conducted the autopsy, agreed with Dr. Spitz that strangulation caused Levin's death.

"It was Jennifer who was pursuing Robert for sex. That's why we wound up with this terrible tragedy." —CHAMBERS' LAWYER JACK LITMAN'S CLOSING ARGUMENT

During jury deliberations, the parties' long sessions in the judge's chambers culminated in a surprise guilty plea. Just before the announcement, prosecutor Linda Fairstein and Chambers' attorney Jack Litman were at the bench flanked by court officers. Robert Chambers at right. ILLUSTRATION: RICHARD TOMLINSON/CHANNEL 5 NEWS/*THE RICHARD TOMLINSON COURTROOM DRAWINGS COLLECTION*, JOHN JAY COLLEGE OF CRIMINAL JUSTICE

After nine days of deliberation, it seemed the jury was stuck. Then suddenly it was all over. An angry-looking Chambers pleaded guilty to first-degree manslaughter, accepting a 5 to 15 year sentence. Seeming near tears, he initially tried to avoid saying aloud to Judge Bell the words required to make the plea legal. After three attempts, the judge finally elicited his reluctant admission that he "intended to cause serious physical injury to Jennifer Levin," thereby causing her death.

To Ellen Levin, Linda Fairstein "succeeded beautifully at keeping Jennifer's spirit alive in the courtroom."

Chambers served the maximum 15 years and was freed in 2003. He and his girlfriend Shawn Kovell subsequently struggled with addiction and Chambers served 100 days for heroin possession in 2005. After pleading guilty to possessing and dealing cocaine in 2008, he was sentenced to 19 years in prison.

IRAN-CONTRA: *The Perils of the Covert and Clandestine*

Early on February 21, 1989, Aggie Kenny sat next to an intriguing-looking man on the shuttle from Washington National airport into the heart of Washington, D.C., en route to the Federal Courthouse. "I didn't know who he was," said Kenny, who was on assignment for ABC News, "but there just was something about him. Perhaps it was the jaunty, urbane-looking cowboy boots he wore while dressed in a business suit and carrying a briefcase."

She thought no more of it and hurried into court for the first day of a trial that would be followed by the nation. Former National Security Council (NSC) aide and ex-marine Lt. Colonel Oliver L. North, a decorated veteran, was being tried on charges related to the Iran-Contra Affair, which the National Security Archives called "the most significant scandal since Watergate."

Millions of dollars in profits from secret arms sales to Iran had been covertly diverted to help the anti-communist Contra rebels overthrow Nicaragua's leftist Sandinista government. Ergo, the label the Iran-Contra Affair. President Ronald Reagan called the Contras "the moral equivalent of our Founding Fathers," and was desperate to see Iranian-held American hostages released.

Kenny was taken aback to see the man from the shuttle enter the courtroom and settle in at the prosecution table. He was independent prosecutor John W. Keker, the former marine and Vietnam veteran heading up the prosecution team.

> "There was much talk about President Reagan's possible complicity in the Iran-Contra Affair." —AGGIE KENNY

North and his bosses, former National Security Advisor Robert "Bud" McFarlane and McFarlane's successor, Vice Admiral John M. Poindexter, were accused of illegally trading arms for hostages and sending government aid to the Contras.

North claimed that when official U.S. aid to the Contras was halted by Congress in October 1984, McFarlane instructed him to find a way to keep the CIA-controlled pipeline moving until aid could be officially restarted. The scandal blew up after records found in the wreckage of a transport plane crash in Nicaragua in fall 1986 pointed to U.S. government involvement. Questions escalated. Newspaper headlines exploded. Aided by his attractive secretary Fawn Hall,

Lt. Col. Oliver North, a decorated former marine, took the witness stand on his own behalf at his April 1989 trial in federal court in Washington, D.C. North's posture was ramrod-straight military-style throughout. Did presiding Judge Gerhard A. Gesell buy North's assertions that he was a pawn on a chessboard? Drawing the judge's inscrutable face on April 6, Kenny simply couldn't tell. He certainly listened intently. ILLUSTRATION BY AGGIE KENNY

North destroyed a paper trail and altered NSC records. He had a document-shredding "party"—held just hours before a Justice Department search—in which so many documents were destroyed, they jammed the shredder.

That November, President Reagan declared, "We did not—repeat—did not trade weapons or anything else for hostages. Nor will we." He fired North on November 25 and announced Poindexter's resignation. Americans debated whether Reagan was truly in the dark or if he was lying.

Was North a fallen hero and liar, as prosecutors claimed, or a fall guy and sacrificial lamb, as his team claimed?

On March 16, 1988, North, Poindexter and retired Air Force General Richard V. Secord were indicted on an array of related charges. Later, Secord would plead guilty to one count of making false statements to Congress. He received two years probation. And McFarlane, who entered guilty pleas to four charges, also received two years probation.

in June, 1988, U.S. District Judge Gerhard A. Gesell granted defense requests to sever the trials of former National Security Council aide Oliver North, former National Security Advisor John M. Poindexter, Iranian-American financier Albert Hakim and retired Major General Richard V. Secord. From Left: North attorney Barry S. Simon, Lt. Colonel Oliver L. North, retired Major General Richard V. Secord (back view), Secord's attorney (foreground), Poindexter attorney Richard W. Beckler, former National Security Advisor John M. Poindexter, Albert Hakim's attorney alongside Hakim (extreme right).
ILLUSTRATION BY AGGIE KENNY

"I felt like a pawn in a chess game being played by giants."
—TESTIMONY OF FORMER MARINE LT. COLONEL OLIVER NORTH

On June 8, 1988, Federal District Judge Gerhard A. Gesell granted defense counsel requests to sever the trials of North, Poindexter and Albert Hakim, an Iranian-American financier. Aggie Kenny vividly remembered the day the severance was granted: "There was a certain tension in the air because of the importance of the hearing and the pressure was huge." But North, who always sat with a Bible before him, "never lost his composure then or at any point in the trial."

North's charges included lying to Congress; obstructing an investigation in order to conceal his actions in providing money, weapons and military advice to the Contras between 1984 and 1986; shredding and altering classified documents; and illegally accepting a gift of a $13,800 security system at his Virginia home. He faced a maximum of 60 years in prison and $3 million in fines.

Kenny recalled John Keker's demeanor as being anything but jaunty—very unlike those cowboy boots. He threw in biblical references. And, said Kenny, "He tended to be impersonal and distant. Attending every day, I recall innumerable heated exchanges among the memorable attorneys and Judge Gerhard Gesell. The judge had a fabulously expressive face and large ears and was a pleasure to draw. And I was impressed with the way he effectively moderated flare-ups between the opposing—and very energetic and combative—attorneys and often did so with humor."

Since North claimed he had been following orders from top government officials, his chief counsel Brendan Sullivan subpoenaed President Reagan as a witness. A president had never been compelled to testify in a criminal trial. Judge Gesell ruled that the president's in-person, in-court testimony was not necessary.

North's wife Betsy sat in the front row, her face inscrutable. "She was lovely looking," said Kenny. North's parents, Oliver Clay North and Ann North, were also present. "What struck me most was the amazing yellow hat worn by Ollie's mother, Ann North," she said. "It was so evocative of a bygone era."

"Strange details sometimes stick with you and I was very aware of
Ollie's mother wearing a prim bright-yellow hat." —AGGIE KENNY

Fawn Hall, a media darling, broke up the long parade of men in suits who testified. Kenny will never forget the "shock and awe" that rippled through the courtroom as North's stunningly beautiful blonde secretary made her entrance. "She was drop-dead gorgeous," she said.

"Oliver North's wife, Betsy North, was very pretty, but lacked Fawn Hall's glamour,'" said Kenny. On April 21, 1989, she drew Betsy seated next to her in-laws. Left to right, Lt. Colonel Oliver North's father, Oliver Clay North, North's mother, Ann North, in her distinctive and very formal yellow hat, and his wife, Mrs. Betsy North. ILLUSTRATION BY AGGIE KENNY

Hall had received immunity from prosecution for her testimony and was a reluctant witness against her boss. She cried twice on the stand—first after Judge Gesell roughly reprimanded her for inadvertently interrupting him.

"Fawn's discomfort at answering Keker's questions was apparent," recalled Kenny. "But when Judge Gesell snapped, 'Please keep your mouth shut while I am talking,' she lost her composure. The public reprimand made me feel uncomfortable, as one is when witnessing someone being publicly humiliated. I felt some sympathy for her."

Judge Gesell quickly agreed to Hall's request for a break. She walked out with tears streaming down her face but returned 10 minutes later, composed.

Oliver North's stunning secretary Fawn Hall grabbed headlines with her tears on the witness stand at her former boss's trial. Testifying on March 23, 1989, she grew emotional describing North's patriotism and loyalty. (Years later, she told *Redbook* magazine that she felt she'd been "used" by North: "I was like a piece of Kleenex to him.") When she shed tears after Judge Gesell snapped at her for interrupting him, Aggie Kenny felt empathy for Hall. ILLUSTRATION BY AGGIE KENNY

Hall broke down again when praising North's patriotism and loyalty and when telling Brendan Sullivan about meeting North, Betsy and their four children in 1983. North's firing upset Hall; she thought it unfair.

"I thought she was pretty theatrical, enjoying her 15 minutes of fame," said Kenny, "while at the same time genuinely upset about North's plight."

Her testimony—that she'd altered secret papers explaining North's role in aiding the Contras at his request—hurt his case. But anyone hoping to see North react was disappointed. "He put his military training to use as always," said Kenny. "He was impassive throughout her testimony."

When Robert "Bud" McFarlane testified, Kenny was struck by the drastic difference between his "strong, controlled image as the president's national security advisor and a Bronze Star recipient and the small, nondescript, lackluster figure before us. His bearing was very low-key and his voice sounded meek and defensive."

McFarlane, who later attempted suicide, was clearly fragile and shaky. "I hoped to capture the pathos of a broken man and his vulnerability," said Kenny.

Calm, and at times defiant, North admitted to lying to a congressman in 1986. He didn't feel his conduct was unlawful, however, because he was under orders not to reveal information. He painted himself as a pawn in others' machinations.

"North maintained his military posture during his four days on the witness stand," said Kenny. "He sat ramrod straight and his testimony was confident. He didn't crack. He was a seasoned military man and showed no emotion of any kind that I could see at the trial."

"I was not stepping in—I was brought in. I was told not to tell."
—OLIVER NORTH

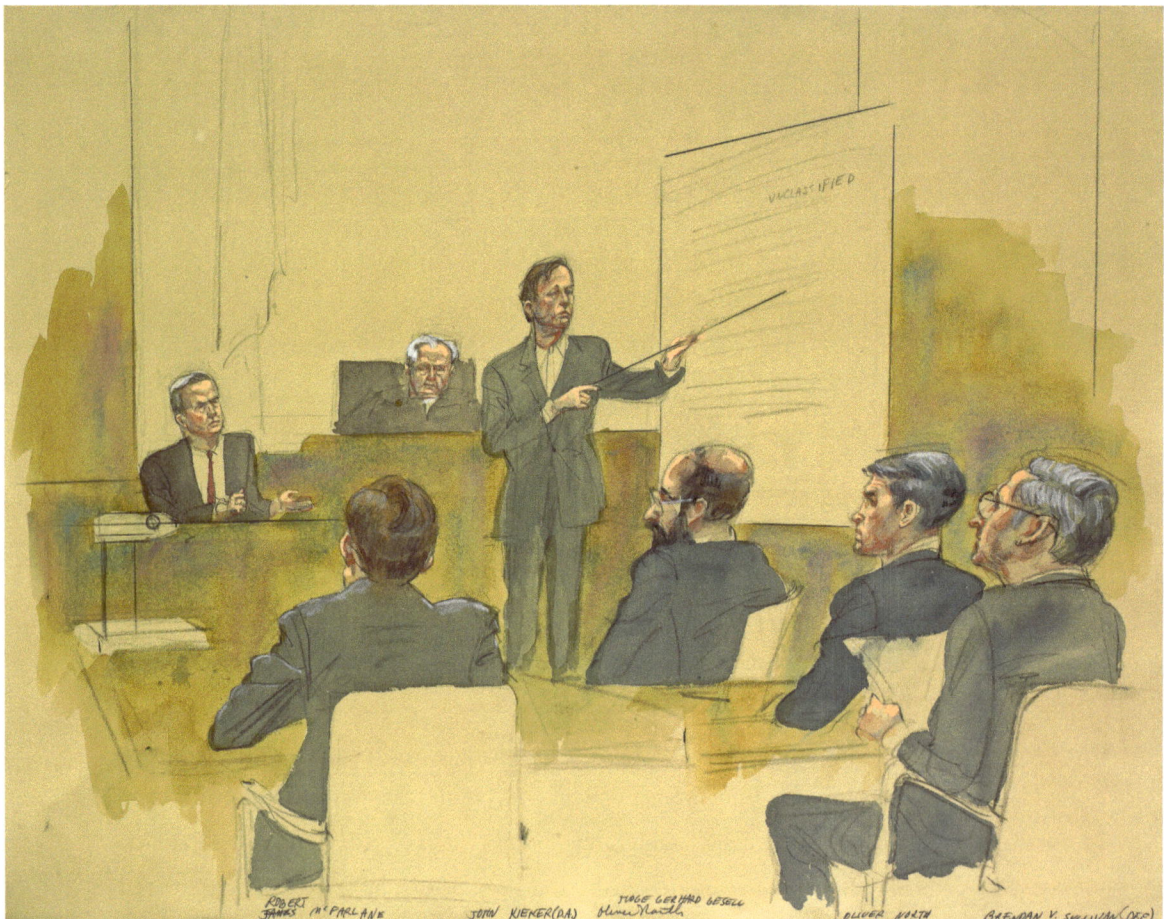

On March 14, 1989, Robert "Bud" McFarlane was questioned by Chief Prosecutor John W. Keker at Oliver North's trial. McFarlane seemed to Kenny "an unglued shadow of his former powerful persona as the president's National Security Advisor and a Bronze Star recipient." Oliver North's defense attorney Brendan V. Sullivan Jr. was seated far right with North second from right. ILLUSTRATION BY AGGIE KENNY

Aggie Kenny attended every day of former Lieutenant Colonel Oliver North's Iran-Contra trial, held in Federal Court in Washington, D.C.—along with a large contingent of domestic and international press. To Kenny, North's chief defense attorney Brendan V. Sullivan Jr. seemed spry and wiry while chief prosecutor John W. Keker seemed rather impersonal and stiff. Kenny particularly enjoyed drawing Judge Gerhard Gesell's "expressive face and distinctive features." As Brendan Sullivan addressed the jury, Keker (foreground) looked thoughtful. North (extreme right) sat beside defense attorney Barry S. Simon. ILLUSTRATION BY AGGIE KENNY

In March 1990, Kenny covered the trial of former National Security Advisor Vice Admiral John M. Poindexter on charges related to lying to and obstructing Congress in the Iran-Contra affair. President Ronald Reagan testified remotely for the defense in that the jury and Poindexter (left) watched his 8-hour deposition on a monitor. The buck stopped with Reagan for his administration's actions. But there was no hard evidence that he knew what was going on—even if he should have known. ILLUSTRATION BY AGGIE KENNY

Closing arguments were bitter. Keker painted North as a habitual liar and claimed that he and McFarlane followed Hitler's strategy: "The victor will never be asked if he told the truth." To an outraged Sullivan, the reference was "sick and twisted."

On May 4, 1989, the jury found North guilty on three counts and acquitted him on nine others. He remained stoic. He was given a three-year suspended sentence and two years probation. The jury, its forewoman later said, believed North was just following orders and got a raw deal. His conviction was overturned on appeal.

Vice Admiral John M. Poindexter, who entered not guilty pleas to five similar charges, stood trial in federal court in Washington, D.C., in March 1990. District Judge Harold H. Greene presided. Poindexter seemed relaxed, puffing on a pipe when he testified.

Chief prosecutor Dan K. Webb said Poindexter deceived lawmakers about arms to Iran to save President Reagan political embarrassment. Reagan, meanwhile, agreed to testify via videotape. His eight-hour testimony was screened for jurors without the possibility of cross-examination—much to the prosecution's dismay.

> "Jurors watched President Ronald Reagan's eerie virtual testimony on a monitor at the Poindexter trial. What better way to distance oneself from a defendant and this mess?"
> —AGGIE KENNY

"I thought President Reagan giving his deposition via monitor a very apt and telling format for his appearance," Kenny recalled. "Testifying remotely, he came across as self-assured."

Poindexter's attorney, Richard W. Beckler, gave a fist-shaking closing argument denying any wrongdoing by his client. He described Poindexter as the victim of a "frame-up story" and noted that the president had said that he wanted the Contras supported. Poindexter was found guilty of five felony counts, including conspiracy and obstruction of Congress. Like North, his convictions were later overturned.

O.J. SIMPSON: *An Infamous "Not Guilty" Verdict, a Civil Justice Coda*

Bill Robles covered parts of O.J. Simpson's racially-charged, nine-month criminal trial in Los Angeles, but spent more time in Santa Monica covering Simpson's civil trial for the wrongful deaths of his ex-wife Nicole Brown Simpson and her friend Ron Goldman. However, Robles spent enough time in both courtrooms to find himself in hot water with both judges.

At the 1995 criminal trial in Los Angeles Superior Court, cameras provided gavel-to-gavel coverage. Robles recalled, "There was an order in place saying 'no likenesses of the jury.'" That meant drawing no close-ups or recognizable depictions of the jury or individual jurors or alternates. So Robles played it safe—or so he thought—drawing them only in outline and showing no facial features.

Yet seeing Robles' work on television, Judge Lance Ito was not happy. Calling Robles' depictions "astonishing in their accuracy," he decided that faces or no, they simply came too close to being recognizable, thus threatening the jurors' anonymity.

> "What Judge Ito saw was like driving from Brooklyn to Manhattan over the Brooklyn Bridge and seeing the skyline. There were no faces." —BILL ROBLES

"Judge Ito thought he saw more than he did," Robles explained. "What I drew was a skyline with hairdos."

Nevertheless, Robles received a subpoena requiring Robles to present himself and all trial art that showed any jurors at a televised hearing at 9 a.m. on April 28, 1995. Robles showed up with CBS media lawyer Beth A. Finley.

"I was the guy of the morning," Robles said wryly. "The lawyers spoke and afterwards, we went into Judge Ito's chambers for a private session. I showed Judge Ito the drawings and he wanted some drastic changes. He wanted me to tone down this and that—the builds of jurors' bodies and any distinctively shaped hairdos. He also told me to put spectacles on some of the characters."

Bill Robles drew this portrait of O.J. Simpson at the former football star's 1996 civil trial. Simpson was found not guilty of the slayings of his ex-wife Nicole Brown Simpson and her friend Ron Goldman at his criminal trial in 1995. But he landed back in court in Santa Monica, California, to fight the victims' families' wrongful death claims. ILLUSTRATION BY BILL ROBLES

On April 28, 1995, Bill Robles went before Judge Lance Ito at O.J. Simpson's criminal trial for drawing the jury in a way that the judge felt rendered them recognizable although they were faceless. Robles subsequently had to have Judge Ito's seal of approval (bottom left) on all art before it could air or be printed. This jury box scene of Robles' passed muster. ILLUSTRATION BY BILL ROBLES

Robles complied: "I toned it down and Ito was very nice. But God, he had mugs and items from all over the world people had sent him. And that courtroom had a revolving door of celebrities going into his chambers. It was amazing."

Under Ito's new system, Robles had to get a stamp of approval on each piece of work from the Public Information Office—more time-gobbling red tape. "And working for CBS with a three-hour time difference to the East Coast really heightened the pressure," he recalled.

Another Judge Ito requirement: no large art pads in court. He didn't want the TV camera to pick them up. "In New York, artists can use great big boards that would never be allowed in court in L.A." Robles explained. "I prefer smaller pads anyway. Less work putting in all the color and faster, too."

Coloring only part of each piece of artwork is also a Robles trademark. "I always like to leave a lot of space in there," he said. "I draw directly with an indelible Pentel Rolling Writer, nothing fancy. No pencil. And I use black. Brown is not dark enough. I also like Prismacolor markers."

"O.J.'s head is larger than average." —BILL ROBLES

Seeing O.J. Simpson in person, said Robles, "I was amazed at how big he was. And from years of football injuries, his walk seemed labored and stiff. But I found it difficult to capture his likeness. To me, he was more unique-looking than handsome. Fred Goldman and his wife and daughter, Kim, were far easier for me to draw. I never did a bad drawing of Mr. Goldman, who had strong features, a great mustache and was very handsome."

As Simpson's infamous "not guilty" verdict in the criminal case was read in the courthouse, Robles watched a monitor in one of the CBS trailers across the street. "They had a city there built on stilts that they called Camp O.J." he recalled. "They expected a racially divided reaction and perhaps a riot and had a police presence with cops on horseback. Everybody was caught up in it."

It seemed inevitable that there would be a wrongful death lawsuit in civil court. And in the fall of 1996, Simpson was back on trial in Santa Monica. A criminal jury must find a defendant guilty beyond a reasonable doubt, but civil trials have a lower standard. Attorneys for the Goldman and Brown families had to prove to the jury only that it was more likely than not that Simpson was responsible for the deaths.

There were some differences in the evidence and the trial strategies, but the witnesses and testimony primarily tracked the criminal trial: the bloody glove, domestic abuse, DNA, blame the victim and witness Kato "Houseguest" Kaelin.

Seeing Simpson at the defense table again, Robles recalled, "There was that air about O.J. like nothing ever happened. He seemed a little on the arrogant side, a little cocky. He wasn't above a little flirting and he would kid around with some of the media outside during breaks."

"O.J. hit on the girl who gave out press passes outside the courtroom at his civil trial." —BILL ROBLES

Robles, however, remained acutely aware of the victims' heartbroken families: "The Goldmans, in particular, were very emotional during both trials. I thought Ron's sister Kim was most poignant of all. I witnessed the family's grief many, many times and I could really feel their pain and emotion. They had a lot to endure.

"Once, during the civil trial, I walked with Mr. Goldman from the parking lot to the Santa Monica courthouse. And when he saw O.J. Simpson in the distance, he said, 'Look at that piece of s***.'"

Robles felt a kind of bond with Ron Goldman's father, Fred, and sister, Kim, that comes along, for an artist, once in a blue moon. "As the lawyers and witnesses held up charts from the coroner and crime scene photographs," he said, "they were crying and holding on to each other. They were good to draw. But it was very emotional. Especially Ron's poor sister, Kim. I remember her sobbing during that testimony."

Fred Goldman, father of murder victim Ron Goldman, wept when he took the witness stand on December 9, 1996, at O.J. Simpson's civil trial. Mr. Goldman spoke of the ongoing devastation of losing his son. ILLUSTRATION BY BILL ROBLES

Judge Lance Ito had become something of a laughing stock at the criminal trial. Critics said Ito allowed Simpson's so-called Dream Team attorneys to ride roughshod over him. But for Robles, the civil trial, which many considered more dignified as a result of Judge Hiroshi Fujisaki's strict, no-nonsense style, turned unpleasant.

That August, Judge Fujisaki had banned broadcast and still cameras—and artists, too. He said artists could sit in court and then draw outside, working from memory. But in October, after an appeal by several news organizations, a California appellate court modified his orders. No cameras, but artists would be allowed in court—though likenesses of jurors or potential jurors were still off limits.

Robles was soon in trouble with Judge Fujisaki. "A news producer and bailiff had come running out of the courtroom to find me," he said, "shouting that the judge wanted me in his courtroom immediately. Walking in, I felt kind of numb and as if it was all a bit surreal. The full impact didn't hit me until later when I was outside answering questions from reporters."

Robles said the incident that got him ejected was a misunderstanding and that he'd inadvertently drawn a very loose impression of a juror. Robles, who had submitted the illustration to Judge Fujisaki for his approval, said, "I don't recall any face on the juror." But there was no room for discussion. "Do you not understand English?" Judge Fujisaki snapped, as Robles tried to explain himself. Robles was unceremoniously kicked out of court.

"Of course I was worried," Robles said. "Not being able to work on this huge trial, let alone my huge loss of income and perhaps a blow to my career? It was a shock."

Eventually, Judge Fujisaki let him back in.

"The media petitioned to get me back in the courtroom. I think it took around a month. Then I was back in court, drawing like it had never happened," Robles said. "In retrospect, I felt Judge Fujisaki was very rude and insulting to me. He was totally lacking in warmth and humor. Judge Lance Ito, on the other hand, was very friendly and respectful of my years of work."

The civil jury held O.J. Simpson liable for the deaths of Nicole Brown Simpson and Ron Goldman and ordered him to pay a $33.5 million judgment. While the verdict had great meaning for the victims' families, it was hollow in terms of its impact on Simpson's pocket.

"Of course, they weren't motivated by money," said Robles, "but they couldn't touch Simpson's NFL pension, and he didn't pay one penny."

In September 2007, Simpson was back in handcuffs in a different case. He said he was just trying to recover personal belongings from sports memorabilia dealers; the authorities said he went too far. A Las Vegas jury convicted him in December 2008 of robbery, assault with a deadly weapon and kidnapping, He was sentenced to 15 years.

Judge Hiroshi Fujisaki presided over the 1996 wrongful death case against Orenthal James Simpson brought by the families of victims Nicole Brown Simpson and Ron Goldman. The trial was held in Santa Monica, California. Nicole's sister, Denise Brown, is at left, the defendant is top left. In the foreground, Ron Goldman's father, Fred Goldman, is seated next to his daughter, Kim Goldman. IL-LUSTRATION BY BILL ROBLES

MARTHA STEWART: *Domestic Diva in Hot Water*

Domestic goddess and business mogul Martha Stewart was in trouble. She stood accused of securities fraud and making false statements to investigators; she faced up to 20 years in prison. She entered not guilty pleas to charges including conspiracy and obstruction of justice and went on trial at Manhattan Federal Court in New York City on January 20, 2004.

In a high-profile case, the stakes are high for artists, too. Elizabeth Williams knew she had to secure a well-situated courtroom seat.

"I wanted—and got—the seat at the extreme right of the front row where the artists sit," she said, "because I knew that from there I could at least get a side view of the lawyers speaking at the podium with Martha seated at the defense table. Sometimes I was craning my neck to see the witnesses between the heads of the jurors. There was no perfect seat in that courtroom as in most courtrooms, so you just did the best you could."

Stewart's problems began with her suspiciously timed sale of 3,928 shares worth approximately $232,000 in the biotech firm ImClone—founded by her buddy Sam Waksal. Prosecutors believed the December 27, 2001, sale was prompted by insider information Stewart should not have possessed. The next day, ImClone stock plummeted, following an announcement that the FDA had rejected ImClone's cancer-fighting drug, Erbitux.

Prosecutor Karen Patton Seymour contended that former Merrill Lynch brokerage assistant Douglas Faneuil, acting on the instructions of his boss, Peter Bacanovic, tipped off Stewart that Waksal was trying to unload his own ImClone stock. Stewart, a former stockbroker, was accused of knowing Waksal's plans to sell. She denied it.

Stewart's dented reputation, potential loss of freedom and ultimate downfall looked set to hinge on a lie prosecutors alleged she told—all to conceal what amounted to a modest $45,000 profit.

Initially, Faneuil, 28, stood behind Stewart's and Bacanovic's claims that they had a pre-existing arrangement to sell Stewart's ImClone stock if it fell below $60 a share. But in June 2002, he changed his story. He said he had informed Stewart of ImClone's impending fall and Waksal's actions and that on Stewart's say-so, he'd made the trade.

Facing the music: after domestic goddess Martha Stewart crashed and burned, Elizabeth Williams attended her trial at Manhattan Federal Court on Centre Street in New York City. She drew her seated at the defense table, listening intently to all the testimony. "In this illustration I tried to capture the dichotomy of Martha: pretty mixed with power," said Williams. Stewart was charged with conspiracy, making false statements and obstruction of justice. ILLUSTRATION: ELIZABETH WILLIAMS/NEWSDAY

Martha Stewart's defense attorney Robert Morvillo delivered a powerful opening statement as her trial began on January 27, 2004. He used a graphic that he hoped would show the jury how little she benefited financially from selling her ImClone shares. U.S. District Judge Miriam Goldman Cedarbaum (right) and Stewart (left) hung on Morvillo's every word.
ILLUSTRATION: ELIZABETH WILLIAMS/NEWSDAY

His boss Peter Bacanovic's attorney argued that Bacanovic was not involved and that Faneuil took it upon himself to tip off Martha, trying to be "the big man."

For Stewart, the cover-up was worse than the crime. Williams, however, was looking forward to drawing a striking-looking defendant, a former model with a great sense of flair, color and style—or so Williams thought. Stewart turned out to be a disappointment.

"Alas, no glam Martha," Williams remembered. "Her clothes were always plain and rather drab. Martha's beautiful head of hair was a hallmark. And at least she came to court every day with it perfectly blown out—or it certainly looked that way even when she sometimes arrived looking a bit windblown. She didn't eschew makeup entirely and she had nice Birkin handbags that cost five figures. But I was definitely hoping for more glamour.

"Perhaps that was for the benefit of the jury—to look suitably serious—but for an artist, given her stylish public image, it was a real let-down. Fashion lover that I am, I was especially bothered that she wore shoes with big thick heels. Not very attractive.

"Martha is quite stunning, but I found her quite tough to draw. She's a very beautiful woman but she is very powerful and tough at the same time." She was stoic, expressionless and completely composed throughout the trial. "And because she didn't show much emotion, I didn't have much to work with there, either."

> "She's very controlled emotionally. Occasionally she had these
> pained expressions when the prosecution spoke."
> —ELIZABETH WILLIAMS

Williams had her coveted front row corner seat but she still had a struggle.

"I don't think it was deliberate," she said, "but Martha seemed to shield herself by sitting between her lawyers and looking down a lot. She rarely walked outside the well of the courtroom. I got my best glimpses of her during breaks. She occasionally turned to chat with her supporters or share her green tea drink with them. Ever the hostess, she once came to court with an L.L. Bean duffle bag full of handmade seat cushions for her court guests and family. Those wooden benches get pretty hard after a while.

"I spent a lot of time waiting patiently for her to turn so I could get a really good look at her. Once or twice, she glanced towards the rows where the press and artists were seated and gave a slight smile. And that's when I got a chance to really study her face. Going in and out of court, she was flanked by bodyguards—we called them Team Martha—to buffer her from Martha-watchers and the public."

"It was a stressful time. I went days and days thinking I was never going to get her." —ELIZABETH WILLIAMS

Star prosecution witness Douglas Faneuil spoke of Martha Stewart's rudeness. Ann Armstrong, Stewart's personal assistant, sobbed while testifying about receiving her first phone call from Stewart after Christmas. Recounting Stewart's gift—a plum pudding—she broke down completely, necessitating a recess.

She was loyal, but Armstrong nevertheless testified to taking a message from Bacanovic on December 27, 2001, warning that ImClone stock was about to collapse.

Prosecutors claimed that Stewart not only spoke to Faneuil that day and then sold her shares, but also later lied about it and doctored her log of phone messages.

"Armstrong testified that Martha went over to her [Armstrong's] computer and pushed the delete button and deleted the message about Bacanovic," said Williams. Armstrong said that her boss then had her reinstate it. But under questioning from Stewart's attorney, Robert Morvillo, Armstrong said Stewart had never asked her to lie or conceal the truth.

"Ann Armstrong was a very powerful witness in swaying the jury without meaning to be," Williams recalled. "She had no reason to testify against her boss other than being compelled to by the U.S. attorney's office."

Williams recalled the media's careful preparations in early March as the verdict drew close: "The TV networks had their producers in the courtroom—with red and black squares of paper they could hold up to indicate guilty or not guilty—and their correspondents waiting outside for them to come out."

"You had to be the first one on air with the verdict."
—ELIZABETH WILLIAMS

U.S. District Judge Miriam Goldman Cedarbaum read the verdict: Stewart was guilty on all four counts. Peter Bacanovic was convicted of all but one charge against him. "You could almost hear a pin drop in court," said Williams, "except for the rustling of the reporters' pens and papers."

OPPOSITE PAGE, TOP: In early February 2004, Elizabeth Williams drew the government's star witness Douglas Faneuil as he was quizzed by Assistant U.S. Attorney Karen Patton Seymour.

OPPOSITE PAGE, BOTTOM: Martha Stewart's personal assistant Ann Armstrong took the stand on February 9, 2004. An emotional witness, she memorably cried when recalling talking about Stewart's Christmas gift to her: a plum pudding.
BOTH ILLUSTRATIONS: ELIZABETH WILLIAMS/NEWSDAY

AnnEArmstrong

Martha Stewart and Peter Bacanovic were convicted on four charges apiece in March 2004. Stewart was back in court for sentencing on July 16 and read a statement to Judge Miriam Cedarbaum. She could have received up to 20 years in prison but was given 5 months behind bars, 5 months of house arrest and a $30,000 fine. ILLUSTRATION: ELIZABETH WILLIAMS/NEWSDAY

Stewart's daughter Alexis slumped in her seat and cried. But true to form, Stewart held her head high and showed little reaction. "She just sat there and stared at the jury and slightly shook her head," said Williams.

Returning to court for sentencing on July 16, Stewart got five months of incarceration, five months of house arrest and a $30,000 fine. Williams decided to focus on just one illustration.

"I made that decision," she recalled, "because it was going to have to be shot and transmitted immediately. So what would that moment be? And when Martha stood to read her statement that was it."

In October, Stewart was quietly admitted to Federal Prison Camp Alderson (or Camp Cupcake, as the cushy facility is known to former inmates) in West Virginia. Stewart later told *Vanity Fair* magazine that her inmate nickname was "M. Diddy."

MICHAEL JACKSON: *Troubled Idol*

Bill Robles hesitated when asked which famous face he most enjoyed illustrating—but ever so briefly: "I have so many favorites in every category but my favorite celebrity would have to be Michael Jackson." Robles shared a few bonding moments with the pop icon while covering Jackson's 14-week trial in Santa Maria, California, in 2005. Jackson was acquitted on all counts after facing charges of molesting a 13-year-old boy, giving him alcohol and conspiring to hold the boy and his family captive.

"I still use the business card I had made with Michael and his attorney Thomas Mesereau on it," said Robles. "I have several celebrity image business cards and when given a choice, most people pick the Michael Jackson card."

The case, a grueling ordeal for Jackson, was a professional triumph for Robles. A huge story internationally, the trial was covered by press from 34 countries, dwarfing even the O.J. Simpson media blitz. Repeatedly, Robles was struck by the passion, adoration and loyalty of Jackson's fans outside the courthouse.

"I saw fans from Spain—girls—in the audience for the entire trial," he recalled. "The head of the European fan club, a guy in Holland, e-mailed me and wanted to meet me. The whole thing was crazy."

Jackson struck Robles as relatively relaxed at first. "In the early days, he sometimes did stretching before court began," he recalled.

"During a break one day, one of Jackson's lawyers took me up to meet Jackson to show him a drawing I'd done of him standing with his three attorneys as the jury entered the courtroom. Upon seeing it, he just lit up like a Christmas tree. He'd seen that one on TV and loved it.

"That encounter just blew me away. Michael was a bit shy and soft-spoken with me. He was very humble and I found him a very warm and gentle person. From that point on, things changed. While Michael used to sit facing straight ahead, suddenly, he seemed to be presenting me with more favorable positions and angles to draw. I started getting a better view of him. At least I did for a while . . .

"I knew the pressure was getting to him. You could see him change, becoming more and more stressed out. It really took its toll on him. He became totally rigid, like a statue."

Michael Jackson wore a different outfit every day at his trial in Santa Maria, California, on child molestation and related charges in spring 2005. Notably, Jackson once arrived in court in his pajamas. ILLUSTRATION BY BILL ROBLES

A young accuser of Jackson's spent four days on the witness stand in mid-March 2005. Robles drew the boy—minus all identifying facial detail—as he was questioned by Jackson's lawyer, Thomas Mesereau. Santa Barbara Superior Court Judge Rodney Melville presided. ILLUSTRATION BY BILL ROBLES

Jackson's accuser was a recovering cancer patient who at age 13 held hands with Jackson in the 2003 documentary "Living with Jackson." Jackson's highly controversial comment about sharing his bed with boys—as an innocent and loving act of friendship—did not help him. Santa Barbara County District Attorney Thomas Sneddon alleged that Jackson and his associates, fearing repercussions, had engaged in a criminal conspiracy to kidnap the child and his family to force them to create a positive video and undo the damage done.

Before the alleged molestation, the accuser's family made a video calling Jackson a "father figure" and "the coolest guy in the world." Jackson's lead attorney, Thomas A. Mesereau Jr., conceded that there were earlier allegations in 1990 and 1993, but noted that Jackson always denied wrongdoing. There had been no charges and no settlement, but the accusations lingered.

In 2005, a parade of witnesses bolstered Mesereau's portrayal of the boy and his family members as "con artists, actors and liars" trying to exploit Jackson's well-known concern for children.

Whether the children are victims, accusers or witnesses, kid gloves are mandatory at any trial involving minors. As usual, Robles did not draw them: "I'd draw the faces of adult witnesses then leave it to the client to decide whether or not to blur them. I drew no likenesses whatsoever of the young witnesses."

"It struck me as funny. With all the hi-tech digital equipment
in the world, these folk are still dependent upon me, my $20
drawing pad and my pen and colored markers." —BILL ROBLES

To Robles, the most riveting witness was Jackson's former wife, Debbie Rowe, who testified for the prosecution.

"The prosecution kept their composure," he said. "But boy, her testimony must have been completely contrary to their expectations because she only had good things to say about her ex-husband. She was great to draw. She made a compelling portrait. She has this strong chin and is very Germanic looking; a real Brunhilda type."

Michael Jackson's former wife Debbie Rowe—mother of his daughter Paris and son, Prince Michael—took the witness stand on May 3, 2005. She was called as a prosecution witness but startled many by speaking well of Jackson rather than criticizing him. ILLUSTRATION BY BILL ROBLES

Famous defense witnesses included Jay Leno, who was quizzed on his interactions with the accusers when the boy was receiving chemotherapy. Leno was asked if he'd been approached for money. He said he sent the boy a "Tonight Show" hat, a T-shirt and a signed picture.

Comedian Chris Tucker, who called the accuser "cunning," testified that he introduced the child's family to Jackson but then became wary and warned Jackson about them. Tucker gave the family approximately $1,500. With these witnesses, Mesereau aimed to show a pattern of the accuser and his family chasing dollars from celebrities.

Celebrity witnesses included angelic-looking "Home Alone" movie star Macaulay Culkin, comedians George Lopez and Chris Tucker and famed late night television host/comedian Jay Leno. On May 24, 2005, Robles drew Jackson looking on as Thomas Mesereau questioned lantern-jawed Leno. ILLUSTRATION BY BILL ROBLES

Although Robles loved drawing Jackson, his distinctive nose and prominent, gaunt-looking cheekbones were challenging. "Luckily, he had that big hair that almost covered his features," he said, "because I had to be spot-on or people would have noticed and complained immediately."

Robles trashed drawings he didn't feel were up to par and started over. He also utilized a trick that served him well when covering the first-ever palimony case that involved 1960s tough-guy movie star Lee Marvin.

"Marvin had unusual proportions," he said. "He had a long space between his nose and top lip. And eventually I had to look at him like a caricature to get it right and overemphasize the proportions a little. It worked well so I sometimes used a similar approach with Michael Jackson."

With time, Robles found that capturing Jackson's iconoclastic look and spirit came more easily. Still, it was a difficult trial. The few media seats in court left artists playing musical chairs. Two would take shifts in a front row seat but when a third appeared, one artist at a time was

A creative way to illustrate the jury while protecting its privacy. As Michael Jackson's trial began, Robles drew jurors working diligently, notepads in hand. On May 4, the day the defense rested, a lineup of eclectic juror footwear spoke volumes about their increasing ease in the courtroom. ILLUSTRATION BY BILL ROBLES

dispatched for a spell to the overflow media room. The press's lair had a jovial atmosphere, but Robles wasn't happy watching the proceedings via fuzzy images on a closed-circuit monitor. He had difficulty seeing all the little details so crucial to his work.

As the trial drew to a close, Robles couldn't tell which way the verdict would go.

> "You're concentrating so intensely, you can't think about the verdict. But when the jurors came in, I thought he was going down." —BILL ROBLES

"The jurors didn't even look at him. They were stone-faced. As the verdicts were read and we heard 'not-guilty,' 'not guilty,' Michael didn't move a muscle. Then he did pull out a hanky and do a little blotting. His female lawyer started to cry, too. She was very emotional."

Jackson's death four years later shocked Robles. "It was so sudden, it was breathtaking," he recalled. "I live close to the University of California Los Angeles, so I could see and hear dozens of TV news choppers hovering over the hospital. It was a very eerie feeling, being so close to this tragedy. It stunned us all."

On June 13, 2005, defendant Michael Jackson was as still as a statue when the verdict was read. As he heard "not guilty" read for each count, tears of relief flowed. Robles captured Jackson quietly drying his eyes. A female member of his camp in court also was overcome with emotion. ILLUSTRATION BY BILL ROBLES

BILL ROBLES' "MICHAEL JACKSON TRIAL" SCHEDULE

The media nicknamed the grueling Jackson trial schedule—three 10-minute breaks and no lunch—the "Melville diet," in honor of Santa Barbara County Superior Court Judge Rodney Melville. I strictly limited my coffee intake and drank just enough water to swallow a morning vitamin, then that was it for the day. I had plenty of incentive. Anyone who left the courtroom outside the three scheduled bathroom breaks was not allowed back in until the next recess. For a working artist, being shut out would have been disastrous.

TASKS OF THE DAY: Check Jackson's attire for military-style stripes or crests and medallions and scrutinize the buttons on his trademark vests. Then, decide what to draw. One Jackson illustration is a given, plus I drew everyone who took the witness stand and the judge and the attorneys.

8.30-9.45 A.M.: Work feverishly on one or two drawings using pen and markers on vellum.

FIRST 10-MINUTE BREAK: Add finishing touches. Run outside with the drawings flapping around in the breeze. If time permits, make a pit stop to try to clean up my hands with soap and paper towel after smudging permanent marker on vellum. Post the artwork onto waiting easel in media tent.

Watch while TV cameras and still photographers from the world's media outlets line up to shoot it for television and print. The days when 28 national and international media representatives shot my work for their respective outlets were the best I've ever had in my career, financially and professionally.

REPEAT PROCESS: By the time we wrapped up at 3:30 or 4 p.m. each day, we were all completely drained. It's far more exhausting than you realize.

DAY'S PRODUCTION TALLY: 6-8 drawings. A drawing approximately every 90 minutes.

BERNARD MADOFF: *America's Most Vilified*

It was widely alleged that disgraced financier Bernard L. Madoff bilked thousands of victims out of more than $64 billion with his grandiose Ponzi scheme. Prosecutors and investigators came to believe that dollar amount was greatly inflated, but getting a final tally proved impracticable. Madoff confessed his crimes to his two sons and on December 11, 2008, surrendered to FBI agents. He was arrested, released on $10 million bail and returned to his luxurious Manhattan penthouse.

Early in January 2009, prosecutors learned that Madoff had violated his bond by secretly giving more than $1 million worth of assets like jewelry to friends and family. But judges continued to decline requests to revoke his bail.

Everything changed on March 12 when Madoff entered guilty pleas to 11 criminal charges, including fraud and money laundering. Two events encapsulated the day for Elizabeth Williams. First, seeing Madoff, 71, handcuffed at Manhattan's Federal Court and carted off to jail. Second, an emotional victim's reaction to her artwork outside court:

"She kissed her fingers then touched the illustration of Madoff in handcuffs and said, 'That's just what I wanted to see!' I said, 'Yes, and that's why I drew it.' The cameraman was a bit upset, though, since we were on a tight deadline and after the interruption, he had to start shooting all over again." Madoff was later sentenced to 150 years in prison.

Bernard Madoff stood with his attorney Ira Sorkin after pleading guilty. He was then handcuffed and led out of the courtroom into the lock up. Many of his victims were seated behind him in the audience. March 12, 2009. ILLUSTRATION BY ELIZABETH WILLIAMS

Madoff victims present in court got their wish on March 12, 2009. His bail was revoked and he was handcuffed and taken away by federal marshals. "I rushed out," Williams recalled, "and called up my photo editor at Associated Press and said, 'I have a present for you! I got Madoff going into the lockup in handcuffs.' I was the first artist to get that image and it showed up everywhere." ILLUSTRATION: ELIZABETH WILLIAMS/ASSOCIATED PRESS

Victims: Dominic + Ronnie Sue Ambrosino   Bernie Madoff Sentencing   6/29/09

Victims Ronnie Sue and Dominic Ambrosino spoke out at Madoff's June 2009 sentencing. "Madoff's facial muscles twitched but he sat stoically facing the judge," said Kenny. She covered the hearing for the newspaper *Metro*. Kenny noticed that when a procession of tearful victims read statements describing "their resulting horror and destitution, Madoff neither looked at nor acknowledged them. I was really struck by their plights. Many had considered themselves Madoff's friends. It was heartbreaking." He was sentenced to 150 years. ILLUSTRATION BY AGGIE KENNY

PART III: ALL THE WORLD'S A STAGE

TERRORISM IN THE HOMELAND

The 1993 terrorist bombing of the World Trade Center's underground parking garage was an ugly foreshadowing of far worse to come. Elizabeth Williams, who drew Islamic extremist suspect Mohammed Salameh at his arraignment, is a resident of Lower Manhattan. "I personally felt the reverberations from the 1993 bomb," she said. "I was across the street when it went off, having just left the World Trade Center concourse."

After any act of terrorism on American soil, court artists face stepped-up security—metal detectors and even, at times, bomb-sniffing dogs sweeping courtrooms. "I lived through 9/11 and my home is near the New York Stock Exchange Red Zone," said Williams, "with all kinds of security and bomb-sniffing dogs and big metal gates. This is how we must live now in New York City; both remembering and trying to forget and get on with our day-to-day lives." Here are just five of the accused and convicted terrorists the artists have drawn. The most recent, Sulaiman Abu Ghayth, became the closest relative to Osama bin Laden ever to face a terrorism-related criminal trial in a U.S. court.

On March 4, 1993, Elizabeth Williams drew the late night arraignment of Mohammed Salameh in Manhattan Federal Court. He was the first Islamic extremist charged in the February 1993 bombing of the World Trade Center's underground parking garage. Terrorists detonated a yellow Ryder truck packed with explosives, causing a blast that left a crater several parking levels deep. Initially, it was assumed to be an accident, not an act of terrorism. The explosion killed six people and injured more than 1,000. "In court, Salameh was seated between a defense lawyer and translator," said Williams. "He looked particularly angry, and I knew it was really important to capture that emotion." Ultimately, Salameh received a 240-year prison sentence.

ILLUSTRATION: ELIZABETH WILLIAMS/NEWSDAY

THE OKLAHOMA CITY BOMBERS:
TIMOTHY MCVEIGH & TERRY NICHOLS

Prior to 9/11, 1995's bombing of Oklahoma City's Alfred P. Murrah Federal Building, which killed 168 and injured more than 500, was the worst terrorist attack in U.S. history. Bill Robles was stunned by what greeted him in Oklahoma City at a joint court hearing for accused bombers Timothy McVeigh and Terry Nichols. "The security surrounding them," he said, "including a caravan of SWAT personnel in SUVs protecting their ground transportation, was almost breathtaking. Being involved in a huge history-making event like that was extraordinary." Robles drew the accused on October 2, 1996, during their sole joint court appearance. Prosecutors claimed they'd plotted the bombing together. But defense attorneys successfully argued to sever their cases. The former army buddies, who faced federal murder, conspiracy and explosive charges, ignored one another. "McVeigh was portrayed as some kind of monster by the media and there was such an aura surrounding him and the hearings," said Robles, "that it was almost surreal. I got an almost demonic quality from him, probably based on the horrible crime, the hype and the heavy security. McVeigh seemed to chat with his attorney a lot. Nichols rarely moved or showed emotion." Nichols received life without parole. McVeigh was executed in June 2001.

ILLUSTRATION: BILL ROBLES/CBS NEWS

Despite Bill Robles' mad dash to the Los Angeles airport, he missed his flight to Helena, Montana, to cover the April 1996 arraignment of accused "Unabomber" Theodore J. Kaczynski for CBS News. Robles and a radio reporter flew to Spokane, Washington, then drove a rented car all night through the Rocky Mountains, arriving in Helena by 7:30 a.m. Kaczynski, a former university professor turned elusive mail-bomb terrorist, lived in a remote explosive-filled shack. Over 18 years, he caused three deaths and injured 23 others. When arrested, he looked like a wild man. But cleaned up for court, Robles felt he was "more of a Christ-like figure and looked anything but menacing. I liked the long hair, beard and orange jumpsuit combo. Something visually interesting is a turn-on." Fifteen minutes after the hearing began, it was over. Robles later drew Kaczynski in a Sacramento court—the city where he committed his final fatal attack. He was sentenced to life in prison.

ILLUSTRATION: BILL ROBLES/CBS NEWS

THE TIMES SQUARE BOMBER:
FAISAL SHAHZAD

Faisal Shahzad tried to detonate a car bomb in Manhattan's Times Square. Elizabeth Williams drew him as he was sentenced to life without parole in federal court on October 5, 2010. Shahzad struck her as both defiant and remorseless. When he stood to address District Court Judge Miriam Goldman Cedarbaum, the Pakistani-born U.S. citizen declared, "Brace yourselves because the war with Muslims has just begun," and, "Consider me the first droplet of the blood that will follow." "You have to have a split-second news sense and I knew his statements would be a key part of the story," said Williams. The defendant threateningly wagging his finger at the judge was another must-have moment. "That was a rare sight," she said. "It was definitely a unique scene I felt compelled to capture."

ILLUSTRATION: ELIZABETH WILLIAMS/ASSOCIATED PRESS

OSAMA BIN LADEN'S SON-IN-LAW:
SULAMAIN ABU GHAYTH

On March 8, 2013, Elizabeth Williams drew Osama bin Laden's son-in-law Sulaiman Abu Ghayth in Federal Court in Manhattan. Through an interpreter, Abu Ghayth entered a not guilty plea to the charge of conspiring to kill U.S. nationals. He was seized in Turkey, then flown to the U.S. rather than to Guantanamo Bay to face a 9/11-related criminal trial. On September 12, 2001, Abu Ghayth, bin Laden's mouthpiece, appeared in celebratory videos with bin Laden, supported al Qaeda's mission and threatened that "the storms shall not stop, especially the Airplanes Storm." Judge Lewis A. Kaplan presided over the 15-minute hearing just blocks from Ground Zero in lower Manhattan. (In 1972, Kaplan was a lawyer for Jacqueline Onassis, then battling paparazzo Ron Galella.) "Abu Ghayth looked very well coiffed with a nicely groomed beard and hair," said Williams, "which struck me as incongruous for this terrorist mouthpiece. Clearly, he was concerned with his appearance. Unlike Mohammed Salameh and Faisal Shahzad, he showed no emotion." He was convicted in March 2014.

ILLUSTRATION: ELIZABETH WILLIAMS/ASSOCIATED PRESS

LEGAL EAGLES: *The Power Players*

Trials can be truly mesmerizing, as engrossing as great theater. And the wildly diverse legal eagles featured in this chapter and throughout this book—many larger than life—are but a tiny sampling of the great legal minds to impress our artists. From Linda Fairstein, a trailblazing former sex crimes prosecutor, to civil rights lawyer William Kunstler. From David Boies and Theodore "Ted" V. Wells Jr. to Harvey Miller and Johnnie Cochran. Meet six they have found especially memorable.

WILLIAM KUNSTLER: CHAMPION OF CIVIL RIGHTS AND CONTROVERSIAL FIGURES & CAUSES

William Kunstler rarely had difficulty finding the spotlight. In the 1950s and '60s, this New York physician's son made his mark as an activist-attorney in the social justice trenches. Kunstler's clients included Martin Luther King Jr., the American Civil Liberties Union and the anti-segregationist Freedom Riders. In 1966, he co-founded the Center for Constitutional Rights. He also represented the Chicago 7 when defendants including Abbie Hoffman, Tom Hayden and Jerry Rubin were tried for conspiring to incite riots at the 1968 Democratic National Convention.

While the defendants were acquitted on conspiracy charges, five were found guilty of crossing state lines with intent to riot. Kunstler himself got a four-year sentence for contempt of court after repeatedly clashing with Judge Julius Hoffman. But all those sentences were overturned.

Kunstler, by then a household name, represented Bobby Seale and members of the Black Panther Party. Artist Richard Tomlinson drew Kunstler at the New York Panther 21 trial.

The deadly 1971 riot at Attica Correctional Facility in New York started with a prisoner protest against inhumane living conditions; 32 convicts and 10 prison staff died. When 62 inmates were initially blamed and indicted for the killings—almost all of which took place at the hands of troopers and corrections officers fighting to regain control of the prison—Kunstler helped defend them.

He was a tall, wild-haired, colorful and sometimes witty character whom Elizabeth Williams recalled as "somewhat disheveled and having a commanding, resonant, gravelly voice." Aggie Kenny once heard him argue before the Supreme Court: "He had the justices in stitches." In another case, Kenny remembered that when jury deliberations once ran well into the evening, Kunstler "brought his two little girls into the courtroom in Doctor Denton footed pajamas. It was awfully cute." William Kunstler died in 1995 at age 76.

1970   ATTY. WILLIAM M. KUNSTLER

William Kunstler during the New York trial of the radical "Black Panther 21." ILLUSTRATION BY RICHARD TOMLINSON, *THE RICHARD TOMLINSON COURTROOM DRAWINGS COLLECTION*, JOHN JAY COLLEGE OF CRIMINAL JUSTICE

Ted Wells' beat is diverse—white collar criminal defense and complex civil and corporate litigation. But his style is always all Wells. "He is effusive, effervescent, articulate, persuasive," said Elizabeth Williams, "and at times a little bit folksy. He has that common touch. And he is great with the everyman jurors because he makes connections. He can be quite disarming. Sometimes he's almost jocular, which seems to get juries' attention."

Trial lawyers are storytellers and Wells, a litigation partner at Paul, Weiss, Rifkind, Wharton and Garrison LLP, is one of the finest.

When former President Ronald Reagan's labor secretary Raymond J. Donovan and seven construction executives stood accused of defrauding the New York Transit Authority, Wells represented the president of Donovan's construction company. Emerging as lead attorney, Wells delivered a three-day closing argument without notes. When he heard 100 "not guilty" verdicts read out, he wept. The victory made Wells' name.

Wells, whose mailroom clerk mother was a major influence in his early life, has had many high-powered clients, including Merck Pharmaceuticals, Johnson & Johnson, Monsanto, former Dick Cheney aide Lewis "Scooter" Libby and financier Michael Milken.

Williams drew Wells again when he defended Citigroup Inc. against the private equity firm Terra Firma's lawsuit seeking more than $8 billion in damages. Terra Firma's British founder, Guy Hands, bought the legendary but ailing music company EMI in 2007 for $6.8 billion. But Hands claimed that EMI's lender, Citigroup, tricked him into overbidding by falsely representing that there was another bidder. Wells successfully argued that Hands simply made a bad deal and had buyers' remorse.

"Wells is pretty persuasive," said Williams. "He speaks well on his feet and is great sparring over legal issues. David Boies was Terra Firma's counsel and sometimes the court would just fill up with lawyers coming to watch the two powerhouse lawyers face off against one another. It was like Muhammad Ali and Joe Frazier. One day I looked behind me and it was standing room only."

Later, the verdict in favor of Citigroup was overturned. Maybe someday there will be a rematch.

Ted Wells, who represented Citigroup against a claim by the private equity firm Terra Firma, questions its chief Guy Hands. U.S. District Judge Jed S. Rakoff presided. ILLUSTRATION BY ELIZABETH WILLIAMS

When General William Westmoreland, former commander of U.S. forces in Vietnam, slapped CBS with a $120 million libel lawsuit for a 1982 news documentary, David Boies was CBS's counsel. "The Uncounted Enemy, A Vietnam Deception," with "60 Minutes" reporter Mike Wallace, alleged that Westmoreland and other top military brass conspired to mislead the public about U.S. prospects in the war. Artist Richard Tomlinson covered the trial as Boies, an Illinois-born teacher's son, was so effective that Westmoreland dropped his lawsuit mid-trial.

Boies' most painful loss was for presidential candidate Al Gore. When Florida vote-counting proved too close to call in the 2000 presidential election, Boies went to war in the Supreme Court case, Bush v. Gore. George W. Bush, of course, emerged as president.

But the super-bright civil litigator and chairman of Boies, Schiller and Flexner LLP has had plenty of victories. Boies successfully defended IBM against anti-trust action brought by the Justice Department that encompassed a five-year trial. Then, in 1977, the Justice Department hired him to take on mighty Microsoft. Although Microsoft was largely the victor in a four-year battle with Justice, Boies emerged with the accolades. CNNMoney.com wrote that his deposition of Bill Gates "shredded Gates' credibility" and *Vanity Fair* dubbed him "The man who ate Microsoft."

In 2001, Boies won a $512 million antitrust settlement from auction houses Sotheby's and Christie's. In another anti-trust case in 2008, he scored a $4 billion win for American Express over Visa and MasterCard.

To Elizabeth Williams, who has drawn Boies at various trials, Boies is almost professorial. "He is a pretty understated guy; there's nothing flashy about him," she said. "He doesn't raise his voice or rant or carry on. But when he gets up to the podium to make a legal argument he is eloquent and has such a command of the legal issues it's great to watch. He's self-contained and composed."

In July 2013, Boies argued before the Supreme Court in support of gay marriage. The divided court struck down a federal law that denied equal benefits to same-sex couples: a landmark victory for gay rights. It also cleared the way for same-sex marriages to resume in California.

CBS' attorney David Boies in court with General William Westmoreland. ILLUSTRATION BY RICHARD TOMLINSON, *THE RICHARD TOMLINSON COURTROOM DRAWINGS COLLECTION*, JOHN JAY COLLEGE OF CRIMINAL JUSTICE

LINDA FAIRSTEIN: PIONEERING PROSECUTOR AND VICTIMS' ADVOCATE

During Linda Fairstein's three decades with the Manhattan District Attorney's Office, she spoke tirelessly for victims. In 1972, the noted prosecutor was one of seven women among 160 men in the office. In 1976, she was appointed chief of New York County's newly created Sex Crimes Prosecution Unit—the first in the U.S. She became a renowned expert in crimes of violence against women and children.

Elizabeth Williams witnessed Fairstein's tenacity and strength at "Preppie Murderer" Robert Chambers' 1988 trial. "She struck me as a very strong and determined prosecutor," Williams said. "We did not see her softer, more sensitive side, as we would have done if the mother of murder victim Jennifer Levin had testified."

Fairstein created the country's first "cold case DNA unit" and crusaded for laws that made it easier for victims to get legal recourse and easier to prosecute sex crimes. Fairstein, whose father was a doctor and mother a nurse, was responsible for putting many sex offenders behind bars. Her early convictions included a dentist who abused women under sedation and Manhattan's so-called "Midtown Rapist," who had at least 18 victims.

"One of the most heart-wrenching experiences is covering a case involving a young victim," said Williams. "They haunt you. You never forget those victims. I think Linda Fairstein should be commended for her bravery and remarkable dedication to victims of abuse and sex crimes. The inner strength she had to see and work with those young victims and find a way to help them is truly amazing. Fairstein has truly made a difference."

She was a founding member of Mariska Hargitay's Joyful Hearts Foundation, went on to become a best-selling crime novelist. Fairstein, who also spearheaded a campaign against the backlog of untested rape kits across America, was the model for TV prosecutors such as Alex Cabot of "Law & Order: SVU."

Linda Fairstein at the Robert Chambers "Preppie Murder" trial. ILLUSTRATION BY ELIZABETH WILLIAMS

Brooklyn-born bankruptcy attorney Harvey Miller led the bankruptcies of Continental Airlines in 1983 and 1990, and of Texaco Inc. in 1987. In 1990 he was involved in the dissolution of the Wall Street banking firm Drexel Burnham Lambert Inc. when it imploded.

Miller, who grew up in a family that struggled to pay its bills, has been called "a minor deity in his field." Williams drew him representing General Motors during a 2009 hearing on the proposed sale of the auto giant to a consortium of new owners led by the Treasury Department. "Harvey Miller is legendary," she said. "He's the most renowned bankruptcy lawyer in the country."

He also represented the securities firm Lehman Brothers, overseeing its 2008 bankruptcy, an unprecedented event that heralded the global financial crisis. Lehman's controlled demise was likely the most complex such case in history. Miller told FT.com that it was "the largest Chapter 11 case ever filed by billions of dollars. It was traumatic and extremely difficult." "In 2010," said Elizabeth Williams, "I saw him testify during the Barclays v. Lehman lawsuit, describing the initial days of the Lehman collapse. He was visibly upset on the stand. He struck me as deeply concerned about the good of the country."

Harvey Miller questions Fritz Henderson, former CEO of General Motors, on the witness stand in June 2009.
ILLUSTRATION BY ELIZABETH WILLIAMS

JOHNNIE L. COCHRAN JR: ELECTRIFYING SPEAKER

The late Johnnie Cochran's famously soaring oratories aided his successful defense of football legend O.J. Simpson. But there was far more to Cochran's 40-year career. Spike Lee, Sean "P. Diddy" Combs, Michael Jackson and Snoop Doggy Dogg were also clients, but Cochran loved representing the little people—what he called the "No-J's."

In 1978, Cochran, the son of a pipefitter, became the first African-American assistant district attorney in Los Angeles County. He loved civil litigation and police misconduct cases. And he took pride in helping ban the sometimes fatal "choke hold" in Los Angeles law enforcement.

"Of course he was a passionate preacher-style attorney at the O.J. trial," said Bill Robles. "But I felt he was—as they all were, really, at that trial—performing for the television cameras. I found Cochran's work in a case in Santa Ana, California, involving two Black Panthers far more memorable."

Robles drew Cochran in December 1996 when he represented prison inmate Elmer G. "Geronimo" Pratt. Pratt's questionable conviction for murdering a schoolteacher and wounding her husband during a 1968 robbery had become a cause célèbre. Many believed Pratt was framed or otherwise wrongfully convicted.

"I was greatly impressed with Mr. Cochran at that appellate hearing," said Robles. "With his fantastic courtroom skills and his manner. I could definitely see how juries would be swayed by him."

Pratt's conviction and life sentence were vacated in May 1997. Cochran called Pratt's release "the happiest day of my life practicing law." Johnnie Cochran died in 2005 at age 67.

Johnnie Cochran questioning key witness Julius Butler at a 1996 appellate hearing in Geronimo Pratt's case held in Santa Ana, California. ILLUSTRATION BY BILL ROBLES

DIRTY MONEY: *How the Mighty Insiders Have Fallen*

In the rich and reckless 1980s, Ivan Boesky, who inspired Michael Douglas' character Gordon Gekko in the movie "Wall Street," was the so-called "King of Insider Trading." He also memorably told UC Berkeley students, "You can be greedy and still feel good about yourself."

But Boesky didn't fall alone. By February 2012, a sweeping four-year insider trading investigation had seen 60 people convicted, while 240 more suspects remained under investigation.

Raj Rajaratnam, former chief of the hedge fund giant Galleon Group, and his friend Rajat Gupta, former McKinsey & Company CEO, were among the lofty figures toppled. The fall of Rajaratnam's friend Danielle Chiesi, a former beauty queen, also captured plenty of media attention.

IVAN BOESKY:
1980S-STYLE WALL STREET SCANDAL

· Ivan Boesky, the so-called Svengali of stock speculation, became the key figure in Wall Street's 1980s insider trading scandal. The Securities and Exchange Commission alleged he had traded on information from a banker at Drexel Burnham Lambert. Boesky, whom Elizabeth Williams recalled as "gaunt, serious-looking and almost frail, with dyed-looking blond hair and dark circles under his eyes," entered a guilty plea to a charge of violating federal securities laws.

On April 23, 1987, Aggie Kenny drew the arbitrager's sentencing in Manhattan Federal Court by the late federal Judge Morris E. Lasker. She remembered Boesky as "impeccably dressed but a hunched-over little man who looked like a character out of a Dickens novel." He ultimately was sentenced to 22 months in prison for violating federal securities laws. Kenny drew Boesky (third from left) with Assistant U.S. Attorney Charles M. Carberry (far left) and attorney Leon Silverman (next to Carberry).

ILLUSTRATION: AGGIE KENNY/ABC NEWS

RAJ RAJARATNAM: FROM BILLIONAIRE TO CONVICT

Bespectacled billionaire Raj Rajaratnam, co-founder of the Galleon Group, managed its $7 billion hedge fund before he plummeted from "the world's richest Sri Lankan" to a lowly convict. Rajaratnam, 53, traded confidential information gathered from various sources.

Elizabeth Williams drew the defendant watching the jurors. "He appeared interested in their reactions," she recalled. "During the prosecution case, he mostly stared straight ahead or kept his eyes closed. But his demeanor changed when his defense was presented and I wanted to portray that. Once, right out of the blue, he gave me a very nice compliment about my work as he walked past me. Otherwise he kept himself to himself."

In May 2011, despite an estimated $40 million defense, Rajaratnam was convicted on 14 counts of insider trading. He was given 11 years behind bars, the longest-ever sentence for insider trading crimes, and ordered to pay a $10 million fine.

In Williams' illustration, Rajaratnam (bottom row) is flanked by defense team members. In the front row (near display board), second chair Terrance Lynam, far left, and Rajaratnam's lead attorney John Dowd, to Lynam's right.

ILLUSTRATION BY ELIZABETH WILLIAMS

In a flurry of visually dry financial cases, Elizabeth Williams enjoyed illustrating former New Castle Funds LLC analyst Danielle Chiesi, 45. When Williams first saw her in a post-arrest "perp walk" video, Chiesi struck her as haggard, aging and dowdy.

"When I first saw her in court for her arraignment a week later, I was completely shocked." Williams said. "I didn't recognize her. I thought she was a TV reporter with the very blonde hair and short skirt. Suddenly, the idea of Chiesi being a seductress who used her sexuality to help build a network of sources to get information she could funnel to Raj Rajaratnam made sense."

Chiesi and her extrovert flirty demeanor were caught on an FBI wiretap passing illegal stock tips to the Galleon hedge fund co-founder and others. She was charged with conspiracy to commit securities fraud. But her taped words also rang out at Rajaratnam's trial. The former beauty queen turned outspoken femme fatale memorably compared insider trading to an orgasm, saying it's "mentally fabulous for me."

Chiesi was charged with soliciting insider information from tech industry executives. Her former lover Robert Moffat—a married man with an ailing wife—was sent to prison for six months. "He was extremely upset in court," said Williams, "weeping and sobbing while his wife and family sat behind him."

Chiesi also passed information to her former New Castle boss Mark Kurland. Her married lover for almost 20 years, Kurland was sentenced to 27 months.

Chiesi entered a guilty plea and on July 20, 2011, faced her sentence wearing garden party attire. "A pale pink sleeveless shift dress, matching platform pumps so high she could barely walk, and a pearl necklace," said Williams.

Chiesi was sentenced to 30 months in federal prison, ordered into mandatory drug and alcohol treatment, and given 250 hours community service and a $25,000 fine. She had to pay the Securities and Exchange Commission $540,000.

ILLUSTRATION: ELIZABETH WILLIAMS/CNBC NEWS

Elizabeth Williams drew Rajat K. Gupta, 63 (seated right), former managing director of the consulting firm McKinsey & Company and former board member of Goldman Sachs, being formally arraigned on February 7, 2012. Gupta was accused of leaking privileged boardroom secrets to his friend and sometime business partner Raj Rajaratnam.

Elizabeth Williams was struck by Gupta's posture. "He sat with crossed arms and a stern look on his face and appeared defiant," she recalled. "The big difference I noticed was that Rajaratnam's wife only showed up once while Gupta's wife and daughters were at the trial daily. You could tell that they had a very close relationship."

Gupta stood accused of telephoning Rajaratnam after a Goldman Sachs board meeting and tipping him off that Warren Buffet's Berkshire Hathaway planned to help out during the raging financial crisis by investing $5 billion. While the tip reportedly made Rajaratnam's fund $900,000 wealthier overnight, Gupta did not benefit financially.

The first time Williams saw Gupta walk out of the lockup in the magistrate's court "with no tie, no belt, just an open-collared shirt, he looked completely in shock." This illustration shows Gupta's defense lawyer, Gary Naftalis, standing before Judge Jed Rakoff at his formal arraignment.

The disgraced financier was convicted in June 2012. Naftalis then worked hard to convince the judge that Gupta's philanthropic track record meant he deserved leniency. That October, he received a two-year sentence.

ILLUSTRATION: ELIZABETH WILLIAMS/BLOOMBERG NEWS

GUNSHOTS RANG OUT

Court artists brought us scenes of justice being served when Dr. King's assassin James Earl Ray, John Lennon's murderer Mark David Chapman, and President Ronald Reagan's would-be killer John Hinckley came to court. They also took us to the pre-trial hearings of accused Colorado cinema slayer James Holmes. These are just a few of the cases our artists found especially memorable.

High-school dropout and petty criminal James Earl Ray confessed to assassinating civil rights leader Dr. Martin Luther King Jr. on April 4, 1968. Dr. King was shot while standing on a balcony at the Lorraine Motel in Memphis, Tennessee. His death triggered race riots in some American cities and heartache around the world.

After finding Ray's fingerprints on a rifle, a scope and a pair of binoculars, the FBI believed he fired the fatal shot from a nearby rooming house bathroom. Ray was apprehended in June in London, England. He entered a guilty plea in March 1969 and was sentenced to 99 years in prison.

Ray later recanted his confession, claiming he was pressured into pleading guilty by his then-attorney Percy Foreman. On October 29, 1974, Aggie Kenny covered an evidentiary hearing in Memphis where Ray's attorney tried to withdraw that earlier guilty plea so Ray could go to trial.

"At Ray's hearings," said Kenny, "I remember his unruly hair and white socks revealing his legs. He appeared quiet and resigned."

His plea withdrawal request was denied but Ray still maintained his innocence despite offering no evidence to support his claims of a government conspiracy or cover-up.

On June 10, 1977, Ray and six other convicts escaped over the prison wall. Recaptured three days later by prison officials and two tired bloodhounds, he'd been hiding in the woods under a pile of wet leaves. Kenny was assigned to a hearing at the prison after his recapture.

"Drawing him in the makeshift courtroom set-up in a penitentiary was a first for me," she said. "Ultimately, I felt rather as if I was drawing an infamous felon in a school cafeteria."

Kenny sat next to freelance court artist Anna Sailing Sandhu, who married James Earl Ray the following year.

Ray died in April 1998 at age 70.

James Earl Ray in court in Memphis, Tennessee, October 1974. ILLUSTRATION: AGGIE KENNY/CBS NEWS

The world wept when Mark David Chapman, 25, assassinated John Lennon outside his home, the Dakota apartment building in Manhattan. On December 8, 1980, Chapman shot Lennon in the back four times then meekly surrendered. A former psychiatric patient from Honolulu, he was once a Beatles fan with Lennon his hero. But he'd apparently become enraged by Lennon's extreme wealth.

The following day, Richard Tomlinson attended Chapman's arraignment on second-degree murder charges in Manhattan Criminal Court. The court-appointed attorney requested a mental evaluation for Chapman.

"He stood there like a bump on a log," Tomlinson recalled. "Nothing going on in his face. He seemed very bland. I felt very badly about Lennon's death. Sometime in 1972, he and Yoko Ono came to 100 Centre Street to visit a celebrity trial. John saw me drawing them, so he made a small ballpoint pen drawing of him and Yoko, which he then handed to me unsigned. I made a motion for him to sign it and he did."

Aggie Kenny was equally unimpressed by Chapman. "I thought he looked like a sloppy, overweight teenager hardly capable of such a heinous crime. I did notice that he clutched a copy of *The Catcher in The Rye*."

Tomlinson drew Chapman again in early January 1981 when he entered a plea of not guilty by reason of insanity. State Supreme Court Justice Herbert Altman ordered psychiatric evaluations.

"Drawing Mark David Chapman left me feeling nothing really," Tomlinson recalled. "Who was this chubby sick little kid anyway? Not someone you could relate to John Lennon. I don't recall seeing any Lennon fans in court. I was too busy coloring Chapman's sweater orange in watercolor over a charcoal drawing and running outside to find our Channel 5 camera crew to tape it. Then I took a subway ride uptown to the 42nd Street Daily News Building for United Press International to run it on their wire service.

"After they took a photograph of the drawing it was back in my hands. A quick check with Channel 5's assignment desk to make sure their tape was okay—it was—and I got back on the downtown subway and went home. The *Daily News* ran my illustration on the front page with their story about Chapman pleading insanity."

Chapman's team prepared their insanity defense—he was diagnosed schizophrenic—but in June 1981, he entered a guilty plea—guided, he said, by a message from God. He was sentenced to 20 years to life in prison. He has repeatedly been denied parole but he wed in 1979 and is allowed conjugal visits.

1980 MARK DAVID CHAPMAN, JOHN LENNONS KILLER

Mark David Chapman arraignment, December 9, 1980. ILLUSTRATION BY RICHARD TOMLINSON, *THE RICHARD TOMLINSON COURTROOM DRAWINGS COLLECTION*, JOHN JAY COLLEGE OF CRIMINAL JUSTICE

John Hinckley stalked actress Jodie Foster and made a failed attempt to assassinate President Ronald Reagan, authorities believed, hoping to impress her. The president was shot and wounded along with White House press secretary James S. Brady, a police officer and a Secret Service agent on March 20, 1981. Hinckley was found not guilty of charges of attempted murder by reason of insanity. He was confined to a federal mental health facility.

Howard Brodie, who flew into Washington, D.C., for Hinckley's midnight arraignment, recalled: "Hinckley really didn't know what he was doing. He was an insane young man."

Aggie Kenny drew Hinckley at a hearing on April 15, 1987, on a hospital request that Hinckley be allowed an unescorted Easter visit with his family. A psychiatrist testified that Hinckley was no longer obsessed with Jodie Foster or saw himself as a hero for shooting president Reagan.

The hospital rapidly withdrew its request, however, after a psychiatrist reported that Hinckley was pen pals with serial killer Ted Bundy, then on death row. Hinckley also was reportedly romantically involved with a woman who killed her sleeping baby with a shotgun.

At the Easter visit hearing, Hinckley was represented by attorney Vincent Fuller. Federal District Judge Barrington D. Parker presided as Hinckley's loyal parents looked on.

John Hinckley (seated center, with glasses) at his hearing on April 15, 1987. ILLUSTRATION: AGGIE KENNY/ABC NEWS

Former neuroscience graduate student James Holmes stood accused of slaying 12 people and injuring 58 more in July 2012 at a midnight premiere of the movie "The Dark Knight Rises" in Aurora, Colorado. He was also accused of booby-trapping his apartment with explosives and chemicals. Holmes entered pleas of not guilty to more than 160 counts of murder and attempted murder. It was one of the worst mass murders in American history.

When Bill Robles began covering Holmes' court hearings, the defendant had carrot-colored curls. With short brown hair, Holmes was barely recognizable on April 1, 2013, when Arapahoe County District Attorney George Brauchler announced that he would seek the death penalty for Holmes. Attorney Tamara Brady announced the defense team's intention to fight back and its belief that their client was mentally ill.

"Initially, I sat about 10 feet behind James Holmes that day," said Robles, "with his parents sitting behind me, holding hands. When the district attorney told the judge, 'For James Eagan Holmes, justice is death,' it was a pretty chilling statement to hear. Can you imagine how his parents felt at that moment?

"The atmosphere was very sober and there were perhaps nine stern-looking sheriffs in that courtroom. Not only tight security but strict security. I was afraid to blow my nose."

A scheduled trial date of February 2014 was indefinitely postponed to allow for further psychiatric evaluations.

Bill Robles saw a change in accused mass murderer James Holmes while covering his court hearings in Colorado.
ILLUSTRATIONS BY BILL ROBLES

#METOO AND SEX CRIMES
OF THE RICH AND FAMOUS

2017's charges of sexual assault, harassment and rape against movie mogul Harvey Weinstein, following decades of sexual predation, lit a fire beneath the #MeToo movement. It was international news, leading women from all walks of life to call for an end to sexual abuse and harassment in the workplace.

Weinstein's sins had been an open secret in the industry for decades, yet he seemed immune from prosecution. #MeToo brought a sea change, however. And Weinstein's arrest seemed to signal the possibility that Hollywood's notorious "casting couch"—around since the 1920s and 1930s—finally might be destined for the bonfire.

As more and more accusers came forward, both of Weinstein and other A-list media world players like television's Matt Lauer and Charlie Rose, while few saw criminal charges, #MeToo heralded a new era of awareness and attitudes. Notably, in the movie kingdom, Weinstein's fate suggested a possible halt to Hollywood's shameful practice of movie moguls abusing their power over actresses with ultimatums: reject my demands for sexual favors and end your career.

Weinstein became a pariah. In that, he was not alone—witness the cases of financier Jeffrey Epstein and director Roman Polanski to name but two. Polanski still has an outstanding warrant in the U.S. after fleeing 40 years ago when facing criminal charges related to a 13-year-old girl. Like Weinstein, comedian Bill Cosby had a very dark side and in 2018, amidst the #MeToo movement, stood trial on charges related to one of his more than 60 accusers.

Weinstein's eventual criminal conviction delivered some sweet vindication to his accusers who first were humiliated by their encounters with him, then by having to share their lives' most intimate details in court. Many hoped that moving forward, the Weinstein verdict meant that fewer victims would feel compelled to suffer in silence.

ROMAN POLANSKI: STILL WANTED

Bill Robles found film director Roman Polanski a delight to draw during a 1977 pre-sentencing hearing. Polanski faced charges in Santa Monica, California, of raping Samantha Geiner, 13, after plying her with champagne and Quaaludes during a photo shoot. "With his unusual features, his long hair, and his small figure impeccably dressed in a double-breasted blazer, he was fascinating." The "Chinatown" and "Rosemary's Baby" director faced six felony counts including child molestation, rape by use of drugs and sodomy. Those charges were dropped for a guilty plea to unlawful sexual intercourse with a minor. On the eve of his sentencing, fearing the judge might bump up his agreed 42-day sentence, he fled the U.S. An arrest warrant is still outstanding.

Romane Polanski 1977
during his pre-trial in Santa Monica
Bill Robles ©

ILLUSTRATION BY BILL ROBLES

Actor/comedian Bill Cosby appeared in Federal District Court in Manhattan decades before his 2018 criminal conviction for three sexual offenses. When Aggie Kenny drew him in 1997, *he* was the aggrieved. Autumn Jackson, 22, daughter of Shawn Thompson, a fan with whom Cosby had a secret affair in the 1970s, was on trial for trying to extort $40 million from him in return for her silence about allegedly being Cosby's love child. After she threatened to take her story to *The Globe* tabloid, Cosby instructed his attorney to call in the FBI.

In court, the one-time Jell-O spokesman conceded that he had sent Shawn and Autumn Jackson more than $100,000 over the years to buy their silence. He feared that if word got out, it would interfere with his highly lucrative business ventures capitalizing on his wholesome image as a beacon of family and moral values.

Kenny drew Cosby on the witness stand on July 15, 1997. "He was very still and unemotional," she recalled.

Ms. Jackson was sentenced to 26 months for conspiracy, extortion and crossing state lines to commit a crime.

The entire episode eventually paled in comparison with Cosby's precipitous fall in 2018 when he was ruled a sexually violent predator. Through his attorneys, he denied all allegations by the approximately 60 women accusing him of crimes from drug facilitated sexual assault to rape.

Cosby was charged criminally for the first time with drugging and sexually assaulting Andrea Constand at his home outside Philadelphia in 2004. Five other accusers were allowed to testify to having been drugged and assaulted by Cosby to show a pattern of behavior. He was convicted on three felony counts of aggravated indecent assault against Ms. Constand. That September, at age 81, he was sentenced to three to 10 years in state prison. However, in 2021, after serving three years, his conviction was overturned on legal technicalities. He cannot be retried.

Bill Cosby on the witness stand in 1997 during Autumn Jackson's extortion trial. Asserting that Cosby was her father, she threatened to tell her story to a tabloid if he did not pay her $40 million. ILLUSTRATION BY AGGIE KENNY.

JEFFREY EPSTEIN: MALEVOLENT SEX OFFENDER SKIRTS JUSTICE

Considered by many one of the most intractably depraved, pedophilic sex offenders in recent memory, multi-millionaire financier, Jeffrey Epstein, was arrested on July 6, 2019. He stood accused of running a "vast network" of underage girls for sex. He faced federal charges of sex trafficking a minor and conspiracy to commit sex trafficking. Epstein, who had homes in Palm Beach, Manhattan, Santa Fe and Great St. James' Island in the U.S. Virgin Islands, often ferried around his alleged victims in his personal Gulfstream, dubbed "The Lolita Express."

"When Epstein was arraigned in Manhattan Federal Court on July 8, his usually coiffed hair was an unkempt mess," Elizabeth Williams recalled. "He had a very angular face which made getting a likeness easier. He was constantly leaning over talking to his attorneys. They tried everything to get him bail, but the magistrate was having none of that."

Epstein had been convicted of procuring a child for prostitution in 2008, receiving a paltry 18-month prison term. The 13 months he served was further softened with privileges like work release, a personal driver, shopping trips and an unlocked cell door. Although a registered sex offender, he did not learn his lesson and his prolific abuse of minors continued unabated.

For his many victims, his 2019 arrest finally promised justice, but it was not to be. Epstein was found hanging in his cell on August 10 in what the New York City medical examiner ruled a suicide. Had he lived, his trial was tentatively set for mid-2020.

At least one civil suit against his estate continued as did investigations into other players like his former girlfriend and aide, British socialite Ghislaine Maxwell, daughter of late press baron, Robert Maxwell. Maxwell, 60, stood trial in New York in December 2021 on sex trafficking-related charges connected to facilitating and participating in Epstein's abuse of minor girls. She was found guilty on five counts and could face up to 65 years in prison.

Defendant Jeffrey Epstein (above, center) with defense attorney Marc Fernich (at right) during his arraignment in New York on July 8, 2019. In December 2021, Epstein's former girlfriend/aide, Ghislaine Maxwell (below), was convicted on related child sex trafficking charges. Epstein, 66, ultimately escaped his punishment. Reportedly, he hanged himself in his cell.
ILLUSTRATIONS BY ELIZABETH WILLIAMS

HARVEY WEINSTEIN: HOLLYWOOD'S
SERIAL SEXUAL PREDATOR

In February 2020, Harvey Weinstein was convicted in New York of third-degree rape and a criminal sexual act. That made him the first truly major league entertainment industry player accused since the #MeToo movement exploded globally in 2017, to pay dearly with prison time for his very serious offenses.

Weinstein, who had more than 100 accusers, had pled not guilty to a variety of sex crime charges, arguing all encounters involved were consensual. By contrast, a prosecutor bluntly described him as an "abusive rapist" and "predator."

When Weinstein was arraigned he was a formidable six-foot-tall figure and moved without aid. However after back surgery prior to trial, he morphed into a stooped, frail-looking presence. "By the time he was sentenced," Elizabeth Williams recalled, "he had a gray beard, his hair was unkempt, his face was more sunken. He'd aged ten years and was confined a wheelchair."

Weinstein rarely made eye contact with the artists during the trial. "He probably didn't even notice us because we were seated four rows behind him on the opposite side of the room." Williams explained. "But when he was sentenced, we artists were right in his line of sight, seated in the jury box. And he made up for it then. He just stared at me with those dark, beady eyes but with a blank look as though he was looking right through me."

During the trial she had some good fortune regarding getting great angles on Weinstein: "Luckily, he would turn around and drape his arm over the back of his chair to see the coterie of friends seated in the rows behind him. Sometimes he moved into the chair in front of the railing so he could get closer to them to chat."

His defense attorney Donna Rotunno argued that without evidence, prosecutors had created an alternative universe in which her client was a monster. She painted his accusers as women who didn't want to take responsibility for their choices.

Defense attorneys Diana Fabi-Samson and Barry Kamins flank disgraced film producer Harvey Weinstein. "I couldn't miss it when he struck this great pose at the end of the day. It really shows his girth and persona." ILLUSTRATION BY ELIZABETH WILLIAMS

Harvey Weinstein, far left, with victim Jessica Mann, a former actress, on the witness stand in 2020. Ms. Mann testified that Weinstein raped her in a hotel room in 2013. "The witness's position," Elizabeth Williams noted, "with her hand over her face, was fortuitous since the Associated Press puts restrictions on showing faces of victims of sexual assault." ILLUSTRATION BY ELIZABETH WILLIAMS

While the jury was out, Williams picked up on a little noticed detail about Weinstein's appearance. "He was a suspender guy, red to match his tie," she said. "And not nice, wide, fancy suspenders, narrow crappy ones with clips on them. With all his money! Another day, however, he did wear a wonderful pair of buttoned, wide suspenders. While he was pondering his fate, there I was, pondering suspenders."

Williams noticed that his confident mood changed quite dramatically over the course of the trial. When the jury notified Judge James Burke that it was deadlocked on the most serious charges, two counts of predatory sexual assault that carried a maximum sentence of life in prison, they asked to be allowed to present a partial verdict. Judge Burke's response: "Continue your deliberations." The development left Weinstein looking concerned. And on February 24, when he was found guilty of two lesser charges that nonetheless could carry serious prison time, he seemed more stunned than cocksure.

Weinstein with attorneys Donna Rotunno and Arthur Aidala. ILLUSTRATION BY ELIZABETH WILLIAMS

Manhattan district attorney Cyrus R. Vance Jr. praised the women who testified saying that, "Their words took down a predator and put him behind bars, and gave hope to survivors of sexual violence all across the world." "Weinstein looked as if he was seething but somehow resigned to his fate," Williams noted. "Finally, he was led away on the journey back to jail."

By July 20, 2021, Weinstein was in Los Angeles where he faced multiple rape and sexual assault charges involving another five accusers. During Weinstein's arraignment on September 20, 2021 at the Los Angeles County Superior Court, Bill Robles recalled, "I was shocked at how disheveled he looked."

ILLUSTRATION BY BILL ROBLES

R. KELLY: FINALLY FACES THE MUSIC

On September 27, 2021, Grammy Award-winning R&B singer Robert "R." Kelly, 54, was convicted in New York federal court of sexual exploitation of a child, racketeering, bribery and sex trafficking. The resounding guilty verdicts followed more than twenty-five years of swirling allegations of sexual, physical and mental abuse, some involving underage girls as young as fifteen.

While Kelly's list of accusers—girls, women and boys—kept growing over the years, he seemed destined to skirt a true day of reckoning. Notably, he was acquitted in 2008 of charges of creating child pornography despite video evidence showing him having illegal sex with a 14-year-old girl. Repeatedly, Kelly's accusers were written off as groupies and gold-diggers, intimidated and not believed. In the changed climate of 2021, however, it was Kelly's defense that was not believed. Notably, his was the first #MeToo era trial of a Black man with predominantly Black victims.

Elizabeth Williams's job was a real challenge right out of the gate. The raging COVID-19 pandemic meant only the defendant, attorneys, judge and jury were allowed in the courtroom. Williams, like other media and the public, could only view a video feed piped into an overflow courtroom.

"Initially, the principals went without masks," she explained, "but the aggressive Delta variant changed all that. Face coverings allow defendants to hide their expressions, to avoid being drawn. So, I was waiting, waiting . . . until finally Kelly's mask slipped down below his nose. Luckily, I grabbed that image because he subsequently pulled up his mask to sit right beneath his glasses."

Thanks to an enlarged image of Kelly on a screen, she could at least see him clearly. "I got some decent close-ups," she said. "Everything else, the witnesses, the judge, was pretty much a blur. I had to work from blurry lines and shadowy shapes and couldn't see the jury at all. I didn't even know the judge wore glasses until we were briefly allowed in court for the verdict."

Viewed via a video feed into an overflow courtroom, prosecutor Elizabeth Geddes (center front) presented closing arguments in singer R. Kelly's sex crimes and racketeering trial. U.S. District Judge Ann Marie Donnelly presided. Inset: Kelly sat with his defense attorney, Nicole Blank Becker. Media could not see the jury. ILLUSTRATION BY ELIZABETH WILLIAMS

Ultimately, the jury believed the prosecution's "racketeering" charge, finding Kelly guilty of heading a criminal enterprise created to lure girls, boys and women for his sexual gratification. For the five key accusers at trial—plus dozens of others watching intently—the verdicts mean justice and vindication. For Kelly they mean a sentence of 10 years to life. He still faces outstanding sex crime charges in Illinois and Minnesota.

MAY IT PLEASE THE HIGHEST COURT IN THE LAND: *The Supreme Court of the United States*

"The Republic endures and this is the symbol of its faith."
—CHIEF JUSTICE CHARLES EVANS HUGHES LAYING THE COR-
NERSTONE FOR THE MAJESTIC SUPREME COURT BUILDING,
OCTOBER 1932

Starting in the 1970s, Aggie Kenny spent two decades regularly covering the Supreme Court for CBS News and ABC News. She grew accustomed to the high level of formality. Accustomed, but no less impressed. "I never lost the sense of grandeur I felt on entering that magnificent marble building," she said, ". . . albeit through a side door."

In 1975, Kenny was assigned to another venerated location in Washington, D.C.: the imposing Dirksen Senate Office Building near the Supreme Court. She covered the U.S. Senate Committee on the Judiciary's two-day confirmation hearing on John Paul Stevens, nominated by President Gerald Ford to replace retiring Justice William O. Douglas.

Kenny's perch in the Senate hearing room was ideal. "It afforded me an excellent, clear view of Stevens and the senators and witnesses," she recalled. "I was seated close to them and so relieved not to be struggling with distant figures."

Attorney General Edward Levi introduced Stevens, praising his judicial opinions as "gems of perfection." Senator Edward Kennedy pressed the nominee about women's groups' complaints about his voting record. But even he called the choice of the 101st associate justice of the Supreme Court "a real quality appointment."

"Looking back at my drawing of Ted Kennedy now," Kenny said, "I am struck by how strongly he resembled Robert Kennedy's oldest son Joseph P. Kennedy II, whom I once drew at a court hearing."

Kenny watched as Stevens good-naturedly answered all questions. "He was very animated and personable and a pleasure to draw," she said. "I enjoyed capturing the senators' likenesses, gestures and idiosyncrasies in clear and dramatic lighting. I remember two senators puffing away on a cigarette and pipe. And I loved drawing the senators in the awe-inspiring, high-ceilinged, wood-paneled rooms. Architectural details add interest to a composition."

Aggie Kenny illustrated the U.S. Senate Committee's confirmation hearing for Supreme Court nominee John Paul Stevens in December 1975. It was held in the Dirksen Senate Office Building and Justice Stevens' appointment was roundly confirmed. Left to right: Senators John McClellan (Ark.), Edward M. "Ted" Kennedy (Mass.), Philip A. Hart (Mich.), Strom Thurmond (S. Caro.), chairman James O. Eastland (Miss.), Roman L. Hruska (Neb.), Hugh Doggett Scott Jr. (Penn.) and the witness, John Paul Stevens. ILLUSTRATION BY AGGIE KENNY

It was a change of pace from working confined to a small cubicle-style space at the Supreme Court, where the layout and lighting are tricky for artists. But walking down the marble hallways and entering the Court Chamber never fails to heighten her sense of anticipation, said Kenny. The 82-by-91-foot room with towering columns and 44-foot ceilings conveys ceremony, gentility and gravitas.

On September 26, 1986, Kenny was on hand to draw the swearing-in ceremony of the 16th chief justice of the United States, William Rehnquist. Retiring Chief Justice Warren E. Burger officiated. Swearing-in ceremonies are solemn yet lighter than the mood while cases are heard. "The justices were visibly relaxed, smiling and happy," said Kenny, who drew them joining the spectators in applause.

"I was always very conscious of the respect and quiet required of every journalist," said Kenny. "The Supreme Court's rulings affect the way we all live and interact in society and I think this underlies the solemnity we all feel in its presence."

Over time, Kenny settled into a routine. "The courtroom doors open at 9:30 a.m. and the justices appear at 10 a.m. sharp," she said. "You could hear a pin drop as arguments begin and decisions are announced."

The artistic challenges, however, remained unrelenting. While all the justices are visible, she needed opera glasses to view those at the far end of the bench. It was a tall order to include all the justices in her composition while capturing the nine famous faces' likenesses and their expressions.

"The room is not well lit," she explained, "but blinding backlighting comes from the huge, luxuriously draped windows that face us. We are assigned to a cubicle in a small alcove just to the left of the bench. Although it's relatively close to the justices, getting a solid view of them individually can be very difficult. It's also constricting because you're stuck in one area and you can never get a different view."

Returning to the Supreme Court in 2013 after a long absence, Kenny found that between sessions she could adjourn to the new ground floor Press Room—complete with WiFi—located near the spectacular five-story marble spiral staircases. "It's a hive of activity," she said.

Illustrating the current court, she found Justices Sonia Sotomayor and Stephen Breyer easier to study because they were closest to her. "But Justices Clarence Thomas and Antonin Scalia tend to lean back in their high-backed swivel chairs, which can effectively obliterate any view of their faces. And the head of Chief Justice John Roberts and the heads of all those beyond him appear small and indistinct."

She also found security tighter in 2013. Just before entering the courtroom, her portfolio, art materials and pocketbook were scrutinized by a court officer armed with a flashlight. Even so, it's clear that much about the Supreme Court does not change.

Kenny drew the swearing-in of Chief Justice William H. Rehnquist by Justice Warren E. Burger on the afternoon of September 26, 1986. Left to right: John Paul Stevens and Thurgood Marshall. William H. Rehnquist, standing before Warren E. Burger, their hands raised. Justices Byron R. White, Harry A. Blackmun and Sandra Day O'Connor. ILLUSTRATION BY AGGIE KENNY

Over two days in February 1987, Aggie Kenny worked diligently as cases were argued before the U.S. Supreme Court. Left to right: Sandra Day O'Connor, Lewis F. Powell Jr., Thurgood Marshall, William J. Brennan Jr., William H. Rehnquist, Byron R. White, Harry A. Blackmun, John Paul Stevens, Antonin G. Scalia. ILLUSTRATION BY AGGIE KENNY

The Trump era saw a conservative new guard join the Supreme Court: Neil Gorsuch, Brett Kavanaugh and last minute Trump appointee, Amy Coney Barrett. Elizabeth Williams drew Gorsuch and Kavanaugh prior to Barrett's arrival. Like Aggie Kenny, she found the court, "Very impressive, very formal and a little bit intimidating. My biggest fear is always that I might drop something and make a noise . . . any noise! These days, lots of security staff walk back and forth in the aisles. That adds to the court's somber air."

Appreciating every touch of fashion in the courtroom, Williams noted that "I loved the way Justice Ruth Ginsburg wore a special lacy collar around her neckline. And she was so diminutive, it belied her stature as a jurist. Sometimes you needed to strain to see her face behind that huge wooden bench.

"It can also be maddening when some justices lean way back in their very large, looming chairs. Justice Clarence Thomas has a habit of doing that. It can really drive you nuts. You just pray they will lean forward. Some justices—Justice Stephen Breyer for one—can also get very animated and impassioned and you have to somehow capture that, too."

Neil Gorsuch was sworn in on April 10, 2017, filling the spot left by Antonin Scalia in February 2016. Brett Kavanaugh, a controversial October 6, 2018, Trump appointee, filled retiring Justice Anthony Kennedy's spot after weathering allegations he sexually assaulted Christine Blasey Ford in college. After Williams drew this lineup, Amy Coney Barrett, a final Trump pick, succeeded cultural icon Ruth Bader Ginsburg who died September 18, 2020. Barrett was speedily confirmed on October 26. L to R justices: Gorsuch, Sotomayor, Breyer, Thomas, Chief Justice John Roberts, Ginsberg, Alito, Kagan and Kavanaugh. The case before the court: Frank v. Gaos. Attorney Jeffrey Lamken of MoloLamken at podium. ILLUSTRATION BY ELIZABETH WILLIAMS

Aggie Kenny, Bill Robles and Elizabeth Williams outside the federal courthouse in downtown Los Angeles, where they covered the John DeLorean case in the 1980s. PHOTOGRAPH BY ROGER HUBBARD

ABOUT THE ARTISTS

HOWARD BRODIE

The late Howard Brodie is a legend in the news business. Walter Cronkite coined the term Artist-Correspondent for him, calling Brodie "the ultimate journalist whose pen speaks a thousand words." The Oakland, California–born artist briefly attended the California School of Fine Arts. He began covering trials for television in the 1960s, starting with Jack Ruby's arraignment.

Previously, he was a sports illustrator for the *San Francisco Chronicle* and a noted combat artist. He saw action in World War II, Korea, French Indochina and Vietnam, and was awarded a Bronze Star for helping soldiers wounded in the Battle of the Bulge. At age 80, Brodie still rode with the army, illustrating desert maneuvers in California for the Pentagon.

His work is in the Library of Congress and the United States Air Force Art Collection. Brodie was inducted into the Society of Illustrators' Hall of Fame, and San Francisco's Academy of Art University has honored him with the Howard Brodie Residence Hall. Mr. Brodie, a longtime central California resident, passed away in 2010.

AGGIE KENNY

Worcester, Massachusetts born Aggie Kenny won an Emmy for her work on the Mitchell-Stans trial for *The CBS Evening News with Walter Cronkite.* During her many years of covering the United States Supreme Court she drew the Warren Burger Court, the Rehnquist Court and the Roberts Court. Her extensive courtroom work includes the trials of political activist Angela Davis, Oliver North and Manuel Noriega, the former military leader of Panama. She has covered cases worldwide for the news media, including the Larry Layton trial in Guyana and the Robert Vesco hearings in the Bahamas.

Kenny's highly-regarded artwork of the World Trade Center responders, *Artist as Witness— the 9/11 Responders,* was exhibited at the New York City Police Museum and the U.S. Senate Russell Building. Her court art has been shown in the Library of Congress exhibition titled *Drawing Justice, The Art of Courtroom Illustration* in Washington DC, John Jay College of Criminal Justice exhibit titled *Rogues Gallery*, the Southern District of New York Federal Courthouse, the New Jersey State Bar Association and the William J Brennan Courthouse in New Jersey.

Her work is in the Supreme Court of the United States collection, the Library of Congress, John Jay College of Criminal Justice Lloyd Sealy Library, and the New Jersey State Bar Association. Kenny was commissioned to recreate courtroom scenes for the 2020 documentary *Tiger King.* She has worked for CBS, ABC, NBC, ESPN, PBS, CNN, *Washington Post, Newsday*, Reuters, Associated Press, *Billboard* and *TV Guide.* Kenny has been profiled in the *Wall Street Journal* and has appeared on WNBC News, WNYC and Fox's *Good Day New York.*

BILL ROBLES

Bill Robles has been a noted courtroom artist, illustrator and portrait artist for more than five decades. The Charles Manson trial in 1970 launched his career as a television news courtroom artist and earned him a special gold medal from the Los Angeles Art Directors Club.

In 1981, Robles was selected by NASA to document the first four space shuttle missions. Numerous clients have commissioned his work for advertising campaigns including: Southwest Airlines, Hilton Hotels, American Express, Capitol Records, and MGM Studios. Robles has been nominated for Emmy Awards for his courtroom artwork. He received three gold medals from the Broadcast Designers Association and awards from the New York and Los Angeles Society of Illustrators. In 2003, the Society of Illustrators of Los Angeles honored him with its prestigious *Lifetime Achievement Award.*

Robles has been featured on *CBS Sunday Morning,* the BBC, CNN, *Crime Watch Daily*, and NBC. He has also been profiled in *Artists Magazine, Los Angeles Magazine, Communication Arts Magazine,* and *Benchmark Magazine London.*

His courtroom work has been represented in the following exhibits: *Drawing Justice: The Art of Courtroom Illustration* at the Library of Congress in Washington DC, *Portraits of Justice* at the United States Federal Court for the Southern District of California in San Diego, the Los Angeles County Law Library, the University of Southern California and the Newport Beach Public Library.

His work is in the permanent collections of: the Library of Congress, the United States District Court for the Southern District of California, and the Ronald Reagan Medical Center at UCLA. He received his B.A. from the renowned Art Center College of Design, where he later taught illustration. For 23 years he also taught drawing at Los Angeles Trade-Technical College Visual Arts program.

His clients include CBS News, CNN, NBC News, Fox News, the Associated Press, Reuters, and various worldwide media outlets.

A native of Los Angeles, Robles now resides in Brentwood, California.

RICHARD TOMLINSON

Richard Tomlinson was born in Akron, Ohio. He attended the Art Center College of Design in Pasadena, California and the School of Visual Arts in New York. His work has been exhibited at the Museum of Television and Radio, the Society of Illustrators, the Art Directors Club, the American Institute of Graphic Arts, John Jay College of Criminal Justice and Syracuse University. Some of his New Jersey courtroom art is on loan for permanent exhibition at Rutgers University Law Library.

Tomlinson's extensive trial assignments included the Abscam case and *Ariel Sharon v. Time Magazine,* the Central Park Jogger and *General Westmoreland v. CBS*. His client list included Metromedia Television News, Fox Television News and CNBC Business News. He was profiled in *Art in America*, *Newsday* and The Society of Illustrators' magazine, *Illustration*. His entire court art collection has been acquired by New York's John Jay School of Criminal Justice. The longtime Manhattan resident passed away in 2010.

ELIZABETH WILLIAMS

Elizabeth Williams attended Washington University School of Art and graduated from Parsons School of Design. She began her court art career in Los Angeles in 1980, covering the case of the Hillside Strangler Angelo Buono, and the anti-trust trial of *Al Davis* (owner of the Raiders football team) *v. the National Football League.*

Williams's court artwork has been published on the front pages of the *New York Times, Wall Street Journal, USA Today, New York Post, New Jersey Star Ledger* and *Newsday.* She received three New York Press Club awards for her courtroom artwork and drew an award-winning advertising campaign for Winthrop Pharmaceuticals. She also illustrated textbooks for Oxford University Press, has drawn illustrations for ABC Sports, the Los Angeles Raiders and the Ammirati advertising agency.

Her work has been exhibited in juried shows at the Society of Illustrators in New York and Los Angeles. Her courtroom illustrations have also been featured in various exhibits including *Rogues Gallery* at the John Jay College of Criminal Justice in New York, *Drawing Justice: The Art of Courtroom Illustration* at the Library of Congress in Washington DC, *Art and Law Together* at the William Brennan Courthouse in New Jersey, the New Jersey State Bar Association. In addition her illustrations are on exhibit at the United States Federal Court for the Southern District of New York. Her artwork is in the permanent collections of the Library of Congress, the United States Supreme Court, the John Jay College of Criminal Justice Lloyd Sealy Library, the New Jersey State Bar Association and many private collections.

Williams has been interviewed by *CBS Sunday Morning, Good Morning America*, BBC America, *USA Today, The New York Times, The Wall Street Journal,* and *Artists Magazine.* The Oxygen Network profiled her and her career in their *Unsung Heroes* series. Her clients include the Associated Press, CNBC News, PBS *Frontline*, and TMZ. She has also worked for ABC News, CBS News, NBC News, CNN, The New York Times, The Wall Street Journal, the Discovery Channel, and HBO's *Last Week Tonight.* She currently resides in New York City.

Howard Brodie and Sue Russell. ILLUSTRATION BY ELIZABETH WILLIAMS

ABOUT THE WRITER

SUE RUSSELL

Sue Russell is an award-winning journalist and author based in Southern California. Her work has appeared in the *Washington Post, New Scientist, Salon.com, PSmag.com, American Legion, Alternet. org* and *Healthline.com* and in her native U.K. in publications like *The Independent, Daily Telegraph, Sunday Times, Marie Claire* and *Sunday Express* magazine. She writes about criminal justice, forensic science, wrongful convictions, animal rights, missing persons and wildfire fighting, plus health, medicine and women's issues. She is the author of several non-fiction books including *Lethal Intent,* a Pinnacle Books "True Crime Classic" and a biography of executed serial killer Aileen Wuornos, who shot seven men to death in Florida and was executed in 2002. Sue has been featured on the A&E Channel's *Biography,* Oxygen Channel's *Notorious* and the Investigation Discovery Channel's *Deadly Women,* along with CNN, Britain's *This Morning* and *Good Morning Australia.* www.suerussellwrites.com

ACKNOWLEDGMENTS

This new version of the *Illustrated Courtroom* would not have been possible without the support and generosity of Sara Bartlett, Dean of CUNY Graduate School of Journalism, and the editor of CUNY Journalism Press, Tim Harper. Dean Bartlett and Tim Harper gave us the design files of the 1st edition which made this 2nd edition a reality. CUNY Journalism Press created a beautiful award-winning book and we are thrilled to be able to update it. My most sincere gratitude to them both.

I would also like to thank artists Howard Brodie, Aggie Kenny, Bill Robles and Richard Tomlinson for their remarkable artwork and dedication to this project. In particular, Aggie Kenny and Bill Robles who spent much time poring over artwork and answering questions to help writer Sue Russell make the manuscript brilliant. To Sue Russell my co-author and colleague, I cannot express enough gratitude. You have done an amazing job and committed yourself to this project over the years; I am in awe of your work, remarkable writing and dedication.

Over the years many people have assisted me in one way or another, I am indebted to you all. I am especially grateful to illustrator Ed Sorel. When we met at the Martha Stewart Trial in 2004, he suggested that I create a book of historic courtroom art. That was the beginning of this journey. A special thank you to Barry Rosenthal of the Barry Rosenthal Photo Studio for photographing all of the artwork with such meticulous care and to Roger Hubbard for our lovely group photo. Also a special thank you to the families of Howard Brodie and Richard Tomlinson. Both artists passed away during the process of getting the book published. The families' help allowed Howard's and Richard's amazing artwork to be seen by many.

I would like to recognize two institutions that are significant in the world of courtroom art, The Library of Congress (LOC) and the Lloyd Sealy Library at the John Jay College of Criminal Justice. Both hold substantial collections of courtroom art. The LOC has now acquired a significant portion of the artwork from this book in their collection, *The Thomas V. Girardi collection of courtroom illustration drawings at the Library of Congress.* Sincere thanks to Sara Duke, the visionary catalyst and curator of the massive LOC collection of courtroom art.

The John Jay College of Criminal Justice's Lloyd Sealy Library holds the entire collection of Richard Tomlinson's courtroom artwork along with a selection of Aggie Kenny's and my artwork. Chief Librarian Larry Sullivan and curator Ellen Belcher, who have a great appreciation for this form of artwork, have amassed a significant collection of New York-based courtroom art. My unending appreciation goes to these two fine institutions, thanks to whom this artwork will be forever preserved for the public.

I would like to thank publisher Sara Stratton of Redwood Publishing and Ghislain Viau of Creative Publishing Book Design for the wonderful work they have done updating the book. Also thank you to Laura Ross who has been a longtime supporter of this project and recommended Redwood Publishing to get it done.

A very special thanks to my family: my husband, Gregg, my brother, Bob, my son, Paul, and my daughter, Samantha, for understanding and supporting my dedication to this project.

—EW

Every effort has been made to ensure the accuracy of the artwork's captions. However, with two of our artists deceased and with decades-old cases, this was not always a straightforward task. The authors regret any errors.

www.ingramcontent.com/pod-product-compliance
Lightning Source LLC
Chambersburg PA
CBHW061148030426
42335CB00003B/152